Classroom
Crusaders

· · · · · · · · · ·

Classroom Crusaders

. . . .

Twelve Teachers Who Are Trying to Change the System

Ronald A. Wolk and
Blake Hume Rodman, Editors

Jossey-Bass Publishers
San Francisco

Substantial discounts on bulk quantities of Jossey-Bass books are available
to corporations, professional associations, and other organizations. For
details and discount information, contact the special sales department at
Jossey-Bass Inc., Publishers. (415) 433–1740; Fax (415) 433–0499.

For sales outside the United States, please contact your local Paramount
Publishing International office.

Manufactured in the United States of America. Nearly all Jossey-Bass books
and jackets are printed on recycled paper containing at least 10 percent
postconsumer waste, and many are printed with either soy- or vegetable-
based ink, which emits fewer volatile organic compounds during the printing process than petroleum-based ink.

Library of Congress Cataloging-in-Publication Data

Classroom crusaders : twelve teachers who are trying to change the system /
[edited by] Ronald A. Wolk, Blake Hume Rodman.—1st ed.
    p. cm.—(The Jossey-Bass education series)
  Includes bibliographical references.
  ISBN 0-7879-0014-1
  1. Educational innovations—United States—Case Studies. 2. Educa-
tional change—United States—Case Studies. 3. Educational leadership—
United States—Case Studies. I. Wolk, Ronald A. II. Rodman, Blake
Hume. III. Series.
LB1027.C4699 1994
371.1'41—dc20   94-15536
                                               CIP

FIRST EDITION
HB Printing 10 9 8 7 6 5 4 3 2 1   *Code 9494*

Contents

Introduction

It has become increasingly clear over the past decade that no significant, lasting improvement of schools in the United States is possible without the involvement and commitment of teachers. The reform efforts of the 1980s produced some progress in schools, but far more remains to be done. Many now believe that the best hope for improving our educational system lies in developing a corps of professional teachers who are empowered to lead in restructuring and revitalizing our schools and are rewarded with the compensation and working conditions appropriate for professionals.

The enormous reservoir of untapped energy, vitality, intelligence, and creativity among the country's teachers could well be the most important force for positive educational change. But harnessing that force is a formidable challenge. Considerable evidence suggests that most American teachers are neither receptive to nor ready for the responsibilities that the reform movement would thrust upon them. The great majority, after all, chose to become teachers after spending a dozen years in school classrooms. It is reasonable to assume that they enjoyed the experience enough to want to become teachers. They clearly did not sign on to lead a revolution.

Even those teachers who see the shortcomings of traditional schooling and would favor change find that the grueling demands of their daily work leave little time for leisure, let alone leadership. And they have long since learned that the system does not encourage or reward dissent from the status quo.

A relatively small but growing cadre of teachers in this country, however, feel so frustrated with the current system that they are embracing new ideas, stepping out of their traditional roles, and becoming active in the movement to overhaul American education. These remarkable people are making a difference, but their stories rarely reach a national audience. As the editors of *Teacher Magazine*, we set out to find such teachers and to tell their stories. Our goal was not only to examine what these teachers accomplished but also how they changed in the process; we wanted to portray their struggle and weigh the costs and benefits that inevitably flow from the risky business of leadership.

Each of the twelve chapters in this book previously appeared in *Teacher Magazine*; ten were part of a series on "teacher leaders" supported by the Pew Charitable Trusts. It was our hope that thousands of teachers in schools across the country would identify in some ways with the individuals portrayed—that they would see that the status quo is not immutable, that change is possible, and that risk taking is worthwhile. But the stories told here should interest anyone who cares about American education. For if schools in this country are to be reshaped into vital learning environments that provide our children with the skills and knowledge they need to thrive, it is people such as those profiled here who will lead the way.

* * * * * * *

Not surprisingly, school reform, with its increasing emphasis on the teacher, has spawned a "teacher-leader movement." Its proponents argue that the best way to improve schools and keep high-quality teachers in the profession is to draw on their expertise and create new, authentic opportunities for them to lead. This movement, for example, calls for principals and other administrators to share power with teachers, particularly at the school level. As a result, classroom teachers in many places are now being encouraged to take part in educational decision making, often as lead teachers or master teachers or members of school-based leadership teams.

Such efforts to "empower" teachers should certainly be encouraged; schools can only benefit from moving important decision making as close to the children as possible. But we feel compelled to emphasize here that the educators profiled in this book are not products of this movement. These women and men have not been empowered. To empower is to give or permit, to authorize. These teachers did not wait to be empowered—they acted. Their authority came from their commitment, their willingness to take risks and make sacrifices. Through self-examination, reeducation, and personal renewal, they found their own persuasive voices—and people listened.

For most, the process was neither quick nor easy. Chicago kindergarten teacher Vivian Gussin Paley says this of her early years in teaching: "I didn't have the kind of curiosity I should have had. I just sort of followed along, surviving. I was nice to children, but I didn't wonder a great deal about what we should be doing or how we should be doing it."

Like Paley, many of these teachers passed a number of years "surviving" within the system before they realized (some with the sudden force of epiphany, others out of a gradual sense of frustration) that something was wrong, that there had to be a better way, that the system had to change. Then they discovered how resistant to change schools are. "I had a lot of freedom with my own classroom," says teacher Harry Chaucer of his efforts to improve his public school, "but as soon as I started talking about changing programs or building new courses, as soon as I was outside the structure of the individual classroom, the politics became real sticky, and everybody's vested interests started to rear their ugly heads."

The educators featured in these pages are fighters; they persevered even when things got sticky or ugly. As a result, they have accomplished remarkable things. Still, they are the first to admit that they do not have all the answers. Much of what sets them apart is their willingness to listen, learn, and ask hard questions. They realize that missteps are inevitable when charting new territory, but they learn from mistakes and keep going. "I have to eat what I cook, and sometimes it doesn't taste very good," acknowledges Adam Urbanski, president of the Rochester (New York) Teachers' Association (RTA).

With the exception of award-winning teacher Kay Toliver, the educators we profiled were not selected strictly for their accomplishments in the classroom. We looked instead for teachers who, through speaking out and acting in one way or another, have had a positive impact on their schools, districts, profession, or community: teachers like Bob Peterson and Rita Tenorio of Milwaukee, who started a feisty newspaper to shake up the local education establishment and then went on to create an experimental public school; Nancie Atwell, whose research and writing have inspired educators nationwide; Robert DeSena, who created the Council for Unity to give students in racially divided Brooklyn a place to come together and solve conflicts peacefully; and Christine Gutierrez, who, with the support of a national reform project, is helping create a "break the mold" school in Los Angeles. We included RTA President Urbanski not because he is an elected teacher-leader but because he is a leader among leaders, a union president willing to challenge time-honored labor practices in the crusade to improve schools.

All but one of these stories ran in *Teacher Magazine* over a twenty-eight-month period, stretching from September 1991 to November/December 1993; "Mr. Chaucer Builds His Dream School" ran in September 1990. The articles appear here in the same order and form, for the most part, that they did in the magazine. In May 1993, twelve teachers affiliated with the Coalition of Essential Schools, a reform-minded organization founded by Brown University professor and author Theodore Sizer, sat down with us to discuss education reform. Among other things, they talked about what is wrong with the nation's schools, how to improve them, and why change is so hard. We conclude the book with an edited transcript of that fascinating roundtable discussion.

During the discussion, Cheri Dedmon, a high school teacher in Hixson, Tennessee, told us, "Most teachers feel like the principal has the power. The principal feels like the superintendent does. The superintendent says the school board has the power. So who actually has the power? If we can convince teachers that they have the power to make a difference, then we'll have something to build on."

The teachers profiled in the following pages do not need convincing. Their experiences and examples give us something to build on.

Washington, D.C.   Ronald A. Wolk
July 1994   Blake Hume Rodman

Acknowledgments

We are deeply grateful to the teachers whose stories appear in the following pages. It takes courage to allow a reporter to follow you around, knowing he or she will see you at your best and worst and tell everybody about it.

When we launched *Teacher Magazine* in August 1989, we envisioned an audience made up of people just like the teachers in this book. Most of the existing magazines we looked at treated teachers like tall children who could not make it through a class without a host of tips and teacher aids. We wanted to write for thinking teachers. And we appreciate the hundred thousand or so subscribers who let us do that every month.

We also want to recognize the professional journalists on the staffs of *Teacher Magazine* and *Education Week* who reported and wrote these profiles.

Finally, we extend a special thanks to the Pew Charitable Trusts and its education program director Robert B. Schwartz for a grant underwriting our teacher-leader series.

—R.A.W.
—B.H.R.

The Editors

. . . .

Ronald A. Wolk is the founding editor and publisher of *Education Week* and *Teacher Magazine* and president of Editorial Projects in Education (EPE), which publishes the two periodicals. Before joining EPE, Wolk was vice president of Brown University for ten years. He was also assistant director of the Carnegie Commission on the Future of Higher Education, assistant to the chairman of the National Commission on the Causes and Prevention of Violence, and assistant to the president of the Johns Hopkins University. Wolk earned a B.A. degree (1954) in English from Westminster College in Pennsylvania, an M.A. degree (1955) in journalism from Syracuse University, and an honorary master's degree from Brown University.

Blake Hume Rodman is executive editor of *Teacher Magazine*, a periodical launched in 1989 by Editorial Projects in Education (EPE). Before joining *Teacher Magazine*, he spent four years as a staff writer at *Education Week*, covering the teaching profession. Rodman came to journalism after seven years of teaching in elementary schools. He taught first in the Madera, California, public school system, then at a private school in Nairobi, Kenya, and finally at the Anglo-American School of Moscow. Rodman earned a B.A. degree (1975) in history from the University of California, Davis, where he also completed work for a teaching credential. He later received an M.A. degree (1984) in journalism from the Medill School of Journalism at Northwestern University.

The Contributors

. . . .

Ann Bradley is an assistant editor of *Education Week*.

Karen Diegmueller is a staff writer for *Education Week*.

Daniel Gursky, former assistant editor at *Teacher Magazine*, is a communications associate in the educational issues department at the American Federation of Teachers.

David Hill is senior editor of *Teacher Magazine*.

Mary Koepke, former associate editor at *Teacher Magazine*, is a Washington, D.C.–based freelance writer.

David Ruenzel is a contributing writer for *Teacher Magazine*.

Elizabeth Schulz, former managing editor of *Teacher Magazine*, is a Jacob Javits Fellow at the University of California, Berkeley.

Meg Sommerfeld is a staff writer for *Education Week*.

This chapter originally appeared as an article in *Teacher Magazine*, September 1990.

. . . .

Mr. Chaucer Builds His Dream School

Harry Chaucer

H arry Chaucer does not put much stock in the supernatural. "I'm a science kind of guy," he says. Lately, however, Chaucer has had the feeling that his Great-Aunt Ester is watching over his left shoulder—even though she has been dead for almost thirty years.

It is more than an odd coincidence that the stern face of Ester Gailer has been in Chaucer's mind recently. For, in an almost eerie way, he is following in her footsteps. Dissatisfied with the existing schools in New Haven, Connecticut, in the early 1900s, Gailer founded a grammar school that stressed high academic standards and personal integrity. The well-respected Miss Gailer's School educated the children of the staff at Yale University and others for about forty years, until her death. "She was strict, she was down to business, and she was demanding," says Chaucer, looking at an old photo of Gailer and other relatives, including his grandmother, who taught at the K–6 school.

Now Chaucer is continuing the Gailer family tradition. He has embarked on the demanding, exciting, and sometimes scary adventure of starting a school from scratch. In a tribute to his spiritual mentor, he has even named the secondary school the Gailer School at Middlebury, Vermont. But the schools share more than a name: Chaucer says he is building on the same philosophical base that made the New Haven school successful.

"I used to play in the school as a kid on weekends and holidays," he recalls. "To me, it was a place that was just full of equipment and a half-dozen teachers you could ask virtually any question of. I thought of school as a place where you came and you were able to pursue what you wanted. Everyone was there waiting to help you learn. You didn't just jump on an agenda and follow along with the school curriculum."

Countless teachers have dreamed of starting their own school, but those thoughts rarely go beyond fantasy. For Chaucer, the mounting frustrations of fifteen years as a public school science teacher and curriculum director pushed him from thinking about alternatives to developing one of his own. So this month, after more than three years of planning, the Gailer School at Middlebury opens its doors to ten ninth graders.

Chaucer had not intended to launch the school, which he hopes will eventually serve 150 to 200 students in grades 7 through 12, until the fall of 1991. But when a group of eager parents in a nearby town heard of his plans, they persuaded him to open a year early. Chaucer sees this first year as a test run; he will be doing the bulk of the teaching, refining the ideas he has been contemplating throughout his career.

"I just think there's an awful lot more we could be asking of the kids," he says. "And they could be much more involved in their own education. I've been trying to make something like this happen in the public system for quite a few years, and I've concluded that it's not possible. I had a lot of freedom with my own classroom, but as soon as I started talking about changing programs or building new courses—as soon as I was outside the structure of the individual classroom—the politics became real sticky, and everybody's vested interests started to rear their ugly heads."

Politics may be behind him, but as a private school educator he will have to contend with another sticky force: the marketplace. Already, Chaucer has had to trade some of his identity as a teacher and begin thinking of himself as a businessman; his customers are the students and their parents, who will pay about $5,000 a year in tuition. "I can't afford not to care about them," he notes. "It's not an option. If I don't respond to them, I'm out of business. It's as simple as that."

Chaucer can be sure that the parents of the inaugural class of ninth graders will not be shy about telling him what they think. The parents who persuaded him to open the Gailer School this year are a candid bunch who take an active interest in their children's education. Meeting over a lunch of New England oyster stew at a Middlebury restaurant, they are bluntly critical of the area's public schools. "The bottom line," says Diane Nazarenko, "is that [my son] Damon doesn't believe it's a place to learn anything. He goes about his education outside of the classroom." Fran Putnam, a private preschool teacher, agrees. "It can't be any worse," she says. "You can't get much lower than kids who every day say they don't want to go to school."

The parents' views are colored somewhat by a bitter teachers' strike last year at their children's middle school. But Nazarenko says the strike had little to do with her decision to send her child to Gailer. "We still would have opted for this because my experience is that there is more opportunity for flexibility in private education," she says. "There's the ability for parents to have some kind of say as to what happens in the school." At the Gailer School, Nazarenko plans to be "as active as Harry's interested in having me be."

· · · · · · ·

There is an undeniable risk for everyone involved with the Gailer School—parents, students, and Chaucer. "You're brave people," he tells the parents. "For me, if worst came to worst, I could get another job. You're giving up your money and your child's education for a year." But it is hard not to be captivated by Chaucer's almost missionary enthusiasm for the project. He has obviously thought deeply about education, both in a broad philosophical and historical sense and in the specific ways it will take place at Gailer. (He even kept a journal of his thoughts as he planned the school.) Chaucer loves to talk about the project, and his friendly, straightforward manner makes his message even more convincing.

"I'm really trying to comprehensively rethink school," he explains. "We've set up a series of programs, some of which are highly teacher directed and some of which are highly student directed. We're trying to balance different needs and interests to build a coherent program for the student rather than a potpourri of courses that don't have any particular relationship to each other. There are very specific programs designed for very specific educational purposes."

The most distinctive component of the school is probably its core curriculum. Students at Gailer will not take separate English, mathematics, science, and social studies classes, as such. Instead, they will follow an integrated, interdisciplinary approach that ties all the subjects together. Chaucer says he is especially intent on bringing together the humanities and the sciences, bridging "the ocean" that has traditionally separated them. Ideally, he says, the school will produce scientists who love the literature of Tolstoy and Dickens and poets who understand the second law of thermodynamics.

The "da Vinci" curriculum, as Chaucer calls it, follows a historical thread that will start in seventh grade with the origin of the universe and progress through modern times with the juniors and seniors. In examining the origin of the universe, for instance, students will discuss the cosmological theories typically taught in physics or astronomy courses, but they will also explore mythology, art, music, and other subjects as they relate to the beginning of time. The same method will be used as students progress chronologically through history.

Textbooks will not have much of a place in the school. "I can see them as helpful resources," Chaucer says, "but I would not picture the school having many, if any, sets of textbooks as they're currently used." Chaucer has devoted hundreds of hours to developing the Gailer curriculum, but he considers it "a labor of love" because it will free him and other teachers from the rigid adherence to text-books that can make classes so routine and unimaginative. "I could literally walk into any biology class anywhere in this country right now," he says, "and with a thirty-second consultation with the teacher, I could take over. Just give me the publisher and give me the chapter; that's how structured it is."

The da Vinci program, which will take two and a half hours in the middle of each day, relies on team teaching. Each team of four or five teachers will teach two grades: seven and ten, eight and eleven, or nine and twelve. "This thing is very heavily faculty weighted," Chaucer notes. "Teachers have 100 percent control of the curriculum and instruction." To give the teams enough time to plan the program, the teachers will meet each morning for one and a half hours. This is possible because, while the core teachers are meeting, the students will be working on technical skills such as math, foreign languages, and keyboarding through self-paced study and the guidance of a few teachers who are not part of the da Vinci curriculum.

The Gailer school day also will include small-group seminars each morning for discussion of contemporary issues; an "inquiry," at which the student meets once a week with a teacher on an independent study project; and an all-school fitness program for teachers and students. It is a long day—from 8 A.M. to 4:30 P.M.—but Chaucer needs the extra time to include all the components. There will be none of the usual study halls and breaks between classes that chew up time in most schools.

Computers and writing will also be two key ingredients in the school program. Chaucer's still talking with various computer companies about grant proposals, but his goal is for every student and teacher to have a computer. The curriculum will be developed and updated on the computer using software like the Apple Macintosh's HyperCard. With HyperCard, a person may quickly tap into a topic by grade level, subject matter, or specific unit. There are places to add curriculum notes (reference books on a subject, for example), instructional notes (hands-on demonstrations for a topic), and learning notes (provocative questions students raised during class-room discussions). "The curriculum is literally improved daily by using the computer to do things you just can't do with pencil and paper," Chaucer says. "Computers can link curriculum and instruc-tion, which are so often seen as separate."

Computers can also make writing easier, but they cannot replace it as a tool for developing critical-thinking skills. So Gailer students will do a lot of writing. One of their main assignments in the da Vinci program will be to write historical fiction. They will be asked, for instance, to write about an imaginary early australopithecine family in a realistic setting and to trace their fictitious family's migra-tion through Cro-Magnon times and on to the present day. Over the course of their studies, the students will have written a virtual novel that covers millions of years of history.

Leadership and community service will be emphasized through-out the Gailer program, especially for seniors, who will be expected to take on more responsibility in the school. For example, they will complete intensive independent study and community service pro-jects and serve on the committees that develop the school's policy, curriculum, and disciplinary rules. "We want to help the students learn that they can make a difference in the world," says Chaucer's wife, Andrea Torello, an elementary school teacher who has been active in planning the school. "That's something that's sorely lack-ing today in schools."

College preparation will not be ignored. Twelfth graders at the Gailer School will receive a heavy dose of advanced placement material because Chaucer knows that people will judge the school on whether its graduates get into good colleges. "I expect that they will," he says. "The school's got to be competitive. We can't gradu-ate kids who are ill prepared. If that were the case, a parent would be foolish to send another kid here."

• • • • • • •

Chaucer says he believes the Gailer School "is going to be one of the most exciting places to work in education. It's going to be hard work, but it's going to be extremely rewarding work." Teacher salaries will be comparable with other area public and private schools. "But the psychic rewards will be higher," says Torello, who will also do some of the teaching this year.

When enrollment reaches the 150- to 200-student target, the school will have a faculty of about sixteen, with Chaucer as the "principal teacher." "I'm looking for as much diversity as possible," he explains. "For the core faculty, I want people who are not only excellent teachers but who have also demonstrated mastery in their field outside of teaching. They've got to first of all be learners, real curious people who are just dying to find out what's been happening in social studies over the years while they've been locked up in the science classroom." With the team teaching and interdisciplinary curriculum, he easily foresees a science teacher discussing literature with the students.

He says it is "ludicrous" the way the existing system restricts what teachers can teach. "It gives the students some very misshapen ideas of what it is to be a human being and what it is to be a scholar." He likes to point to Charles Darwin as an example of a true scholar. When Darwin traveled through South America, he studied and wrote about whatever he encountered, whether it was geology, botany, or mining, Chaucer says. "He didn't say, 'I am a biologist, this is my niche, and I'm going to do biology in a narrow way.'"

Although Chaucer is not planning to hire teachers who are just like him, he has clearly considered his own background in developing his demanding requirements for Gailer faculty. His résumé lists an impressive array of teaching experiences. For example, he has taught special education at the Yale Psychiatric Institute and almost every science subject at Champlain Valley Union High School in Hinesburg, Vermont. He holds a master's degree in biology and won the Outstanding Teacher of the Year Award in 1981 from the National Association of Biology Teachers, and he is interested in scuba diving, woodworking, and playing with Legos with his young son.

Chaucer turned forty recently, and he admits there is a relationship between reaching that milestone and tackling this formidable project. "I spent the first chunk of my career working with as many different types of people as possible," he says, "from Head Start–aged people to graduate students to working in psychiatric hospitals and schools for the retarded. The second chunk of my career, I taught as many different content areas as possible, particularly in the sciences. This piece is synthesis, putting it all together and making it work in a whole school that deals with whole kids and a whole faculty in a meaningful way. I think that's sort of a 'fortysomething' kind of thing to do."

* * * * * * *

One big obstacle to starting a new school can be locating an appropriate building and getting it zoned. In that regard, Chaucer was extremely fortunate. He found, and will rent, a former parochial school that has not been used much in the last twenty years. The three-story, yellow-brick school appears a bit humble surrounded on three sides by the stately gray stone buildings of Middlebury College. But it is solid. And the setting could not be much more idyllic: large windows overlook Gailer's four-and-a-half-acre playing fields, complete with hockey rink. Beyond that is the center of Middlebury, perhaps the quintessential New England town, with its church steeples, rustic inns, antique shops, town green, and backdrop of heavily wooded Green Mountains.

The first year, however, the Gailer School will have a temporary home. While the main building undergoes modest renovations, Chaucer and his ten students will meet across the grounds in a convent where the nuns who taught at the old parochial school used to live. One still lives upstairs.

Finding the main building was relatively painless, but it was only one of "a phenomenal number of details involved with starting a school," Chaucer says. A highly abridged list includes obtaining state approval, passing fire and safety inspections, buying various kinds of insurance, advertising, hiring a staff, and developing policy. "In all of these things," he adds, "I'm trying not to simply take the existing model but to question the existing model and look at ways of improving it."

The planning has been demanding and nerve-racking at times, more so than Chaucer imagined. He recalls a typical episode: "One night I woke up at midnight, completely awake, with no chance of getting back to sleep. And I thought, 'What if I don't get any students? What if I hold this party and nobody comes?'"

Money has been a constant worry: how much tuition to charge, how much to pay himself and other staff members, how to pay for equipment such as computers, and how to survive on limited family resources.

To develop the school the way he would like, Chaucer is counting on grants from federal agencies and corporate foundations. He has submitted a number of formal applications and preliminary proposals with the goal of raising more than $500,000. The money would be used primarily to further develop the school and its curriculum. After that, he would like to obtain grants for endowments and scholarship money that would allow Gailer to offer financial aid to a more diverse group of students.

This year, with only minimal rental expenses for the convent building, Chaucer says he can get by on the $50,000 in tuition from his ten students. The largest expense will be salaries for him and four other part-time teachers who will help out.

Still, the costs of the recent months have created a financial strain on Chaucer and his family. All the phone, photocopying, and mailing expenses involved with planning the school have really added up. "But just to be doing something that is a fundamentally creative process has been tremendously rewarding," he says. "I've enjoyed it enormously."

For now, Chaucer has his building, he has some students, and he is ready to see if he can make his dream school a reality. But even after years of successful teaching, he will probably be more nervous than his students on the first day of school. "There's a positive tension that I've never felt before," Chaucer says. "I think that's a good thing. It's going to be a fascinating year." And he hopes Aunt Ester is watching—and pulling for him.

Daniel Gursky

· · · · · · ·

The Gailer School opened, as planned, in the fall of 1990 with ten students. By the beginning of the 1993 school year, the number had jumped to forty-four, with six full-time and four part-time faculty members. Harry Chaucer is now the headmaster, and his wife and partner in the project, Andrea Torello, is the dean.

♦ ♦ ♦ ♦ ♦ ♦ ♦

Lyzbett Long

This chapter originally appeared as an article in *Teacher Magazine*, September 1991.

2

Listen to the Children

Vivian Gussin Paley

Eddie: You know, 353 years ago everyone could see
God. He wasn't invisible then. He was young so He
could stay down on Earth. He's so old now He floats
up in the sky. He lived in Uganda and Egypt.

Fred: That's good, because everyone in Egypt
keeps. They turn into mummies.

Since 1979, Vivian Gussin Paley has been capturing the candid voices of Eddies and Freds in her books about life in the classroom. The Chicago kindergarten teacher shatters the myth that elementary education is about as cerebral as baby-sitting. Remember the old insult, "Teach kindergarten long enough and you start talking like a kindergartner"? Well, say that to Paley, and she would probably take it as a compliment. In her world, kindergartners are the ultimate original thinkers, and kindergarten is a glorious place for the intellectual and philosophical growth of both children and teachers.

Paley also breaks the ageist stereotype that older people are only interested in coasting onto the golf course. She published her first book at age fifty. And in 1989, at sixty, she became the first classroom teacher to win the prestigious MacArthur "genius" award. The honor, bestowed annually on scholars, poets, activists, and scientists—extraordinary thinkers and doers in any field—comes with a cash award and no strings attached. Winners, who are nominated, evaluated, and chosen by mysterious, MacArthur-appointed nominators and committees, get anywhere from $150,000 to $375,000. Paley received a sum equal to about eleven years of an average teacher's salary—a whopping $355,000.

Instead of retiring early on her laurels or taking time off to focus on her writing, Paley is still mixing up the finger paint and setting out the blocks for little people in the classroom.

Who is this teacher? And what is it that makes people think of her as a genius? Last June, I spent a few days with Paley to find out.

• • • • • • •

Just a mile from the shores of Lake Michigan, the private University of Chicago Laboratory School stands like a Gothic castle across a broad, grassy median on the edge of the century-old university campus. Ivy has climbed the school's massive stone walls, reaching all the way to the second-story windows of Paley's classroom.

Inside, the teacher sits at a table, listening to a wide-eyed, wispy little girl tell a story about a family of field mice. Paley writes down every word the girl says, while the other twenty-two children spin a noisy web of activity around them.

"I am bloody!" a boy sings in delight as he oozes red finger paint between his stubby fingers. Others duel with umbrellas, dress teddy bears in doll clothes, plunk on a miniature piano, and bake sheets of cookie-shaped clay lumps in an oven made of giant blocks.

Paley takes the chaos in stride, donned casually in a pair of white cotton slacks, a plain short-sleeved shirt, and her favorite shoes—sneakers. Amazingly lithe and active—only the streaks of gray in her tightly curled hair and the wrinkles around her face speak of age—Paley reminds me of the Arthurian wizard, Merlin, who goes through life backward. Maybe it is the medieval architecture or the magic that the children use to turn clay into cookies, but I have the strange feeling that if I were to come back next year, Paley would actually be a year younger than she is now.

As she moves about the room, I begin to notice another unusual thing about her: she does not smile at the children. And although she is a warm, responsive teacher, Paley does not engage in habitual hugging or hair tousling. My behavior around children is quite different. I start grinning like a carved pumpkin as soon as kids open their mouths. Everything they say just seems so amazing. I have always considered myself an ardent admirer of children, but here, in Paley's class, I suddenly detect a hint of condescension underlying my knee-jerk, "Aren't they cute" response.

Cute is not profound. Cute is just cute.

Paley, on the other hand, gives the immediate impression that "kidtalk" is serious business. As she listens to the children's stories about mice, kittens, sisters, and bad guys, Paley looks truly engrossed, like a cultural anthropologist witnessing the ritual behavior of a previously undiscovered, highly civilized people. She asks questions and comments on their perceptions without a shred of condescension in her voice. She does smile. But she smiles with them, not at them.

It is no wonder Paley is, as Lab School principal Revira Singer says, "beloved" by her students.

Paley's respect for children and her genuine interest in what they have to say are part of her genius. But according to Paley, she did not acquire those qualities until halfway through her career.

As we crunch across the gravel playground to watch her class play on the monkey bars, Paley talks about her career. She talks a lot. But unlike many loquacious souls, she does not quick-fire her words. She bakes them slowly and deliberately. Her deep, husky voice sounds like a cross between Lauren Bacall's and my husband's Jewish grandmother's.

This sharp, intense woman cannot tell her story from beginning to end in one calm, quiet sitting. This is, after all, a school day. So

Paley and I share conversation in snatches, during recess, over lunch, and after school while walking Cass, her dog. The accompanying soundtrack is a wild one, peppered with crows cawing, Cass panting, and frequent interruptions by her favorite people: "Mrs. Paley, can you open my milk?" "Can you tie my shoe?" "Can I go to the bathroom?" "Watch me, Mrs. Paley!"

* * * * * * *

Paley married young and slid into a traditional teaching career without much thought. While raising two sons, she taught in public schools in Louisiana and New York before coming back to her hometown to teach at the Lab School. "I didn't have the kind of curiosity I should have had," she says of her early years in the classroom. "I just sort of followed along, surviving. I was nice to children, but I didn't wonder a great deal about what we should be doing or how we should be doing it."

In the mid 1960s, several experiences woke her up. The country was experimenting: men began wearing their hair long, women began wearing their skirts short, and schools began adding sex education to the curriculum. Paley got caught up in the latter. As part of a pioneering, pilot program, she was asked to teach kindergartners about sex.

The children listened to Paley's lessons. They learned grown-up words like *intercourse, penis,* and *vagina* and what the words meant. But after class was over, the children told outrageous tales whenever they talked about conception and childbirth. Babies come from watermelon seeds, egg shells, and dinosaur bones, they would say, seemingly in earnest.

Paley was astounded. Although the children knew the "real" story, they still preferred their own versions. "Well, I was hooked," Paley recalls. "For the first time in my life, I didn't want to give any answers. I wanted to find out what they thought. I couldn't get enough of it."

At about the same time, a high school science teacher approached Paley with an odd request. His grandchild had just turned five, and he realized that he knew nothing about how little children think. He wanted to sit in on a few of Paley's classes.

Watching the older man interact with children was an inspiration for Paley. Truly curious, he asked open-ended questions and listened to their answers with few expectations of what they would say. "I saw true Socratic and nonjudgmental questioning of children," she recalls.

Through these experiences, Paley began to take her subject—the children—seriously. And it was then that her adventure began.

The best adventures ultimately require one difficult risk: a willingness to look deeply and critically at oneself. As Paley began to listen to children, she also began to hear herself. And she did not always like what she was hearing—about race, for instance.

Schools were becoming increasingly integrated, and Paley's attention focused on racial issues. She began asking herself how well she, as a white teacher, was relating to black children in her class. How, for example, did she react when a black boy wore a "Supernigger" T-shirt to school? How did she feel when another screamed, "I don't have to listen to no white lady!" What should she say when pale-skinned Paul told brown-skinned Alma that she looked like chocolate pudding? What was the right way to behave?

Admitting to herself that she felt awkward with African-American children, she began to examine her feelings and responses. The process of self-evaluation and the discovery of her own biases and shortcomings became the subject of her first book, simply called *White Teacher* (Harvard University Press, 1979).

Paley wrote from the heart, capturing and questioning her experiences in the classroom over a five-year period. Reading it is like perusing a diary.

>   When Valerie told Fred she wanted a white partner, I
>   was silent. I did not know what needed to be said to help

both of them. If she had told Fred his painting was scribble-scrabble, I might have said, "Fred, Valerie thinks you're painting scribble-scrabble. Is that what you're doing?" Then Fred could have told us how he felt. But I could not transfer this matter-of-fact, non-judgmental description of what was being said when race or color was involved. When Denise became annoyed with Valerie and told her not to sit next to her because this was not a "brown" chair, I responded with equal annoyance. "Valerie may sit wherever she wishes, Denise. Please don't tell people where to sit." I saw I was purposely avoiding the part about the brown chair.

Like many whites, Paley had grown up believing that it was impolite to talk about racial differences, to say *black* in front of a black person. Politically correct teachers did not see black or white children—they just saw children. "Color blindness was the essence of the creed," according to Paley.

But she began to wonder how this color blindness affected children of color. By ignoring the unmistakable blackness of her students' skin, was she, in effect, teaching them that there was something wrong with being black? "As I watched and reacted to black children, I came to see a common need in every child," she wrote. "Anything a child feels is different about himself which cannot be referred to spontaneously, casually, naturally, and uncritically by the teacher can become a cause for anxiety and an obstacle to learning."

She began to experiment quite simply, using every chance she had to mention the words *black* and *white*. "Steven, that orange shirt looks good on your brown skin," she would say.

Paley noticed that the more she talked about being white and being black, the less children seemed to attach negative associations to the words themselves. By acknowledging racial differences without using them as the basis of judgment, Paley was learning to demystify race and truly to relate to her students as individuals. Among many other things, she was discovering how to become a better teacher.

It was just the beginning.

. . . .

It is a cloudless Monday in June, and Paley's students have just gone to music class. In the quiet, empty room, Paley walks over to a cupboard and gets out a small, inexpensive cassette tape recorder. "This was the next turning point," she says, holding up the gadget.

The self-evaluative process of writing *White Teacher* set fire to Paley's curiosity. Wanting to be more aware of how she responded in general to children in group discussions, she turned on a tape recorder—and left it running. Pushing the record button changed her life. "My tape recorder did what nothing else could do: give me criticism," she recalls.

She began taping every day and transcribing the tapes every night. Like a rabbi who spends a year pondering one line of the Torah, Paley would analyze the things she said to children. Was she being fair? Was she really listening to them? "I heard the querulousness, the critical undertone in my voice," she admits. "The answer was implicit in my questions, and the children's voices showed that they were looking to see if their answers were 'right.'" Furthermore, Paley noticed that she did not always take the children's questions seriously. Sometimes, she would not even answer them.

Identifying and admitting her own mistakes was just the first step. In a brilliant move—one that is both obvious and unimaginable— she shared her confessions with the children. "I was listening to our conversation on the tape recorder last night," she would say, "and I realized that I didn't really answer that question you asked."

The children were fascinated by these disclosures. "It was as if I had just given them a prize," she remarks brightly. Her willingness to include them in the process of discovery sent a strong message to children: "Everything you say is of prime importance and must be understood by you and me."

The tape recorder, with its wondrous ability to replay, also gave her the time to hear the children's point of view. Her transcripts captured what she calls "high drama" in the kindergarten: philosophical discussions about God, fairies, and robbers, as well as speculative discussions about whether stones melt when they are boiled. Paley presented her discoveries in her second book, *Wally's Stories: Conversations in the Kindergarten* (Harvard University Press, 1981).

> "Whoever sits in the time-out chair will die for six years until the magic spell is broken," [Wally] says one day after a session on the chair.
>
> "They turn into a chair," Eddie decides, "and then God breaks the spell."
>
> "Not God," corrects Wally. "God is for harder things."
>
> "Fairies could do it," says Lisa. "Not the tooth kind."
>
> "It is a fairy," Wally agrees. "The one for magic spells."
>
> The children like Wally's explanations for events better than mine, so I give fewer and fewer interpretations each day and instead listen to Wally's. The familiar chord he strikes stimulates others to speak with candor, and I am the beneficiary.

For several years after completing *Wally's Stories*, Paley turned her attention exclusively to observing and examining the differences between the behavior of boys and girls. And in 1984, her third book, *Boys & Girls: Superheroes in the Doll Corner* (University of Chicago Press), was born.

At first, Paley's new editor thought the book was too sexist. After all, it was full of anecdotes about girls playing with baby dolls, while boys transmogrified into Incredible Hulks and smashed blocks around. "The editor wanted extra material on what I thought should be done to elevate the consciousness of boys and girls," Paley recalls.

But as with her earlier work, Paley preferred to ask questions rather than supply the answers. As always, her probing unearthed more questions about how her own perceptions affected her role as teacher. The book was published as Paley wanted it.

> The boys have been trying to leave the doll corner since they came to kindergarten. They are superheroes now—or feel they should be. . . .
>
> This year, I have tried to examine boys' play with more objectivity than in the past. . . . If I have not yet learned to love Darth Vader, I have at least made some useful discoveries while watching him at play. As I interrupt less, it becomes clear that boys' play is serious drama, not morbid mischief. Its rhythms and images are often discordant to me, but I must try to make sense of a style that, after all, belongs to half the population of the classroom.
>
> It is easier said than done. The further away a boy moves from fantasy play, the more I appreciate him. . . . I seem to admire boys most when they are not playing as young boys play. It is a conflict I must face because superhero play has increased in the past decade and begins at an earlier age.

While working on Boys & Girls, Paley realized that her kindergartners already had developed stereotypical ideas about sex roles. "By age five, the die is cast," she says. "I was getting the end of the story, and I was curious to find out what the beginning was." So she asked to spend a year teaching preschoolers in the Lab's lower school.

Paley ended up staying for six years. There she wrote her subsequent three books: Mollie Is Three: Growing Up in School (University of Chicago Press, 1986), Bad Guys Don't Have Birthdays

(University of Chicago Press, 1988), and *The Boy Who Would Be a Helicopter* (Harvard University Press, 1990).

Once again, as the following excerpt from *Bad Guys* shows, Paley's tape recorder captured the fears, dreams, and logic of the culture of childhood embedded in her students' fantasy play and invented stories.

Though it has taken Fredrick two weeks to mention [his mother's] new baby, his sullen restlessness has already become a classroom fact. He paces the room, glowering, as if expecting a fight, and then sits for long periods at the story table, covering small papers with black crayon marks.

"Do you want to tell a story, Fredrick?"

"I hate stories."

"Well, if you change your mind. . . ."

"All right, I changed my mind," he blurts out, beginning his story quickly.

"A baby cries and the mommy has to go get him. Then she has to snuggle him. Then He-Man tries to hurt the baby but he doesn't. Then He-Man has a fight with every bad guy." He pushes his chair back noisily. "And don't ask me anymore! And don't ask me if I'm He-Man because I'm not! I'm always the baby from now on. And don't ask me!" He runs into the block area and lies down in a house Mollie has just built.

"This is my rainbow house," she says.

"Do you need a baby? I mean, I'm not the baby! I am the baby. Where's my bed? I'm crying and you have to snuggle me. You didn't bring me the blue blanket." He begins to cry.

"Are you really crying, Fredrick?" Mollie asks.

"No! Can't you just snuggle me, Mollie? Can't you bring me the blue one?"

"Here it is, little snuggle baby," Mollie murmurs. "Here's a nice beddy for you. Don't cry." She smooths his hair and covers him with the blue blanket.

"Mollie," Fredrick says calmly. "I'm the new borned person, OK? No father and no brother. Mommy and the baby. Don't let anyone come in, OK?"

Mollie begins to hum "Mmm-mmm. No daddies—no baddies—mmm." She adds more blocks to the house while Fredrick moans and rocks under the blanket.

Over and over, Paley and her tape recorder witnessed fantasy coming to the rescue of children. Words from adults often failed to provide solace, say, to a little boy who was afraid of losing his mother's love; whereas fantasy allowed the child to actually become the baby again, to be coddled and comforted.

As Paley observed the preschoolers, she became convinced that children use stories, make-believe characters, and plots to express their own fears, desires, and doubts. Her students disclosed much more of their feelings as characters in their stories and fantasy play than in any "real" conversations.

· · · · · · ·

Paley rings a brass bell. The children stop playing and pull their tiny chairs into a circle around a large, green rug. Everyone knows the routine for this ritual: it is time to act out the stories they dictated to Paley earlier in the day. The author plays the lead, and the other necessary actors are chosen by counting around the circle.

Onto the green "stage" scampers the wispy redhead who wrote the tale about four newborn field mice. Before Paley can begin narrating, an argument breaks out. It seems that the little mouse has planted her best friends strategically in the circle so that they, and no other children, will be chosen to nibble and squeak with her on stage.

The other children cry rat.

Paley reaches for her tape recorder to capture the ensuing discussion. She is collecting material for her new project, a book about peer friendship and rejection that she is tentatively calling, *You Can't Say, "You Can't Play."*

Not surprisingly, the project began with a kind of confession. "I didn't quite get it right," she says simply. "In the epilogue of *White Teacher,* I say that adults haven't figured out how to live fairly with people but that children figure it out every day in their play." She leans forward, whispering as if sharing a vital secret. "But they haven't yet!"

Children do reject other children, routinely and ruthlessly. "You aren't my best friend," they taunt. "Only best friends allowed in this game." Children set up "no trespassing" signs so strong and clear that even adults hesitate to enter.

"Teachers are not ambivalent about hitting or destroying property," Paley says. "Children know that hitting is not allowed. But a set of behaviors that is far more damaging is rejection. Yet every teacher I know is ambivalent about interfering when it comes to best friendship."

Furthermore, she realized that society puts the blame on the victim. Adults teach the lonely child how to be accepted, never questioning the social skills or responsibility of the group.

Paley decided to intervene by clearly stating that in the very public place of school, rejection is not allowed. Her new line of action is a departure from the patterns of her past. In her listen-and-observe role, she felt it was important to let children figure out how to solve problems their own way. But she now realizes, she says, that "the victim can't wait for the group to decide that it doesn't have the right to do it."

Earlier in the year, Paley banned rejection in her kindergarten classroom. "You can't say, 'You can't play'" became the rule. Since then, she has been filling notebook after notebook with observations and transcribing tape after tape of dialogue on the subject.

The "you can't say" rule has changed a lot of things in the classroom. Paley has witnessed miracles. The smart, pretty girl who was so good at excluding other children that Paley says she could have run a "school for rejection" has become a close friend of the girl she most often tormented. But Paley has also seen problems. Children with power often had a hard time playing by the rule. It is not fair, they insisted. Why could they not choose not to play with someone?

True to form, Paley took their question seriously. So seriously, in fact, that she grabbed her tape recorder and opened the discussion with older children in other classes. "Here's what I'm doing with my kindergartners. What do you think?" she asked. "Is this rule fair?"

"I've really come back to what I started in *White Teacher*," she says. "*White Teacher* was entirely a question of human morality. What is fair? What is right? And how can we discover it? This has become the most important aspect of the classroom and of my writing."

With a bulging satchel of transcripts and full notebooks, she is ready to spend the summer at a country hideaway revisiting the moral landscape of the classroom she and her students have cohabited. At this point, she is not sure what she will find. All she knows for certain is that thinking about the issue is the right thing to do.

· · · · · · ·

Paley sweeps through the room quickly, pushing in chairs, collecting trash, flipping out the lights. It has been a long day in the classroom, but she does not seem tired. She looks ready to begin working.

In a way, that is what she will do. Besides being a full-time teacher, she is, after all, a writer, a runner, a wife, and a grandmother. She is also frequently called on to lead workshops and address educators at conferences around the country.

What does she do, I wonder, compose book chapters while jogging? Write speeches in her sleep? Her energy and intensity seem remarkable enough. But Paley is quick to dispel any superteacher myth. "I'm an ordinary person who has found a focus," she insists.

Paley is also quick to disassociate herself from the genius label. Although grateful for the sense of financial security the MacArthur award has given her, she talks about it in a modest, awkward way, as if uncertain why she was chosen.

So what is it about Paley that is extraordinary? In just one decade of study, she has learned many things about the process of teaching and the culture of childhood. But Paley's genius does not reside in what she knows. After all, the theories and discoveries about teaching and play outlined in her books are fascinating but not entirely new.

Ironically, Paley's brilliance lies in her willingness to admit what she does not know.

And that is no easy feat. Too often, teachers fall prey to the know-it-all syndrome. Perhaps it is natural; the label "teacher" almost implies it. Is not a teacher someone who has knowledge and passes it on to others, someone who has the skills to mold a student's character? Is not a teacher the one who knows the answers?

I remember during my own teaching years being much more interested in focusing on what I was doing right, not wrong. Most of my colleagues seemed to feel the same way. Of course, we were always striving to be better teachers, but we presumed we were basically on the right track.

Paley, on the other hand, presumes nothing. She exemplifies a "habit of self-reflection," says Barbara Bowman, director of graduate studies at the Erikson Institute, a Chicago-based center for the study of young children that recently honored Paley with its annual award. "Vivian simply doesn't accept everything that comes down the pike. As she sees things, she thinks about them."

Paley is constantly observing, analyzing, and evaluating her own actions, unafraid to ask some basic questions: "Is what I say fair?" "Is what I'm doing right?" And she is willing to turn to children for the answers.

"My experience has taught me my enormous fallibility," she says. "It is fascinating to me, not negative. I have learned the incredible effect it has on children when errors are freely admitted and treated only as learning opportunities. And what a wonderful adventure inward it is to keep asking, 'Why am I doing what I'm doing? What does it mean?'"

Mary Koepke

. . . .

Vivian Gussin Paley's You Can't Say, "You Can't Play" *was published to favorable reviews in 1992. Over the 1993–94 school year, Paley took a one-year sabbatical from the University of Chicago Laboratory School to work on yet another book, tentatively titled* A Journey Back to Black and White. *In it, Paley comes full circle, revisiting, with new material, the themes of* White Teacher.

Rob Levine

This chapter originally appeared as an article in *Teacher Magazine*, March 1992.

. . . .

3

Daring to Be Different

Joan Riedl

Marilyn Bue remembers the shock she felt the first time she visited Joan Riedl's classroom in North Elementary School in Princeton, Minnesota. "It wasn't like anything I had ever seen before," recalls Bue, who had a son in Riedl's fifth grade program at the time. "It looked like a beehive, with everyone talking and doing things and moving around. Joan would be talking to just a few students, and it confused me because I thought the whole class should stop and listen to her."

Bue's reaction is a common one. Parents do not know what to make of a learning environment that is radically different from the one they knew as students. But those who visit Riedl's classroom soon see for themselves, as Bue did, that children thrive in the setting she has created.

Riedl's classroom is set up like a resource room. The children are workers, responsible for synthesizing and using rather than just reproducing information. Riedl has relinquished some of her authority, giving her students choices and welcoming their comments about how the class is going.

The elementary school teacher has not always taught this way. A decade ago, a classroom visitor would have found Riedl at the blackboard talking to students seated in straight rows. But in the early 1980s, Riedl began to explore the uses of technology in the classroom. Her quest launched her on a journey. She read extensively, contacted and visited schools using innovative teaching approaches, observed her own students, and thought long and hard about what makes sense. All the while, she was fashioning her own approach to teaching.

Through this process, Riedl has learned that change comes at a price—but that there is a payoff, too. After overcoming some resistance in her school and community, Riedl recently persuaded the local school board to designate her program a "genuine learning alternative"—another name for a school within a school.

But she has set her sights even higher. Under a controversial new Minnesota law, a select number of licensed teachers from across the state will be allowed to design, start, and run eight "charter" public schools under contract with a local school board (discussed later). Riedl wants to be one of them.

• • • • • • •

Smartly dressed in a crisp white blouse with brown twisted beads and a brown blazer, Riedl is describing the way she used to teach. For many years, Riedl says, she was a teacher cut straight from the traditional mold. She would stand in front of her classroom lecturing to children who had textbooks open in front of them. In those days, Riedl says, she made all the decisions in the classroom, and it was always quiet and orderly.

Then, in 1981, her elementary school acquired some computers. Riedl signed one out and wheeled it into her classroom. She put students on it for standard drill and practice and was surprised when they started coming in during lunchtime to use it. "There has got to be more to this machine," she thought. "But I don't know what it is." Seeing that technology had the power to motivate students, she wanted to find out more.

Riedl shopped around for a master's program in technology. After calling universities and telling them exactly what she wanted—a program that would teach her how to use some of the newest technologies as thinking and teaching tools—she settled on the College of St. Thomas in St. Paul. The program, designed for both elementary school teachers and businesspeople, taught those enrolled how to use technology in common sense ways as a natural learning tool.

The St. Thomas program introduced Riedl to the ideas of the software developer John Henry Martin, who created the IBM program Writing to Read. These ideas provided the groundwork for Riedl's re-created classroom. Setting up a classroom as a series of workstations, she reasoned, makes good sense. If a teacher asks students to do real work at these stations and holds them accountable for what they accomplish there, the computer could be more than just something for them to play with after finishing their seat work. At a workshop on Writing to Read, Riedl heard that IBM was looking for someone to train teachers in schools that were implementing the program. After finishing her master's, Riedl took the job.

During her two-year master's program, Riedl had developed a vision for using technology in the classroom. But she found it difficult to translate that vision and transfer her enthusiasm to the teachers she was training for IBM. "The teachers were frustrated," she remembers. "They were thinking, 'Oh god, here are these machines; what am I going to do with them?'" So, after a year of teaching teachers, she decided she needed to return to the classroom and try out computers herself.

• • • • • • •

When Riedl got her own class in 1988, she was eager to make some changes. Technology got the ball rolling, but the transformation did not end there. Riedl realized that to use computers in a common-sense way, other aspects of her classroom would have to change, as well. And the master's program put her in the right mind-set: it started her questioning her old approach. "I had to go away for a while before I could realize how cold my classroom was," she says. "I began to think of my classroom as an artist's palette. I take a bit of this color and bits of that and see if it blends; if it doesn't, I can wipe it out."

Over the next several years, Riedl used her new palette to paint a new classroom. This year, the changes have been more formally recognized by the district. Riedl's fourth and fifth grade class and a third and fourth grade class that follows Riedl's approach have been made genuine learning alternatives within the school. What this means is that parents and students can choose to be part of the program. Still, the program is not independent of North Elementary. It must operate, for example, within the schedule imposed by the larger school.

Riedl once heard a quotation that she says describes the most important shift in her teaching: "Before I was a sage on the stage; now I'm a guide on the side." To get there, Riedl says she had to give up power. "I made it clear that the students' opinions matter," she says. "They know that this is their room."

It is true that students in Riedl's program have more control than most, but they also have more responsibility. Far from being passive recipients of knowledge, Riedl's students are workers, who must learn to manage themselves. Much of the day is spent with the class split up into groups working on projects or at technology "stations." Riedl works with one group at a time and fields questions from other students.

Today is a typical day. In one section of the classroom, a sandy-haired boy peers through a video camera with hand raised, five fingers spread. He signals a countdown: 5, 4, 3, 2, 1. The camera focuses momentarily on a blackboard where "Channel 11 News" is neatly printed. Another boy says, "Welcome to Channel 11 News" as he wheels the board away, which reveals two other boys seated at a news desk. They introduce themselves and take turns giving summaries of the weather and local news.

At another station, four girls have clustered chairs around a videodisc player. One student, the group leader, holds the remote control. The leader asks, "Does everybody have a workbook and pencil?" They answer, "Yes," and she starts a science video clip.

At the language arts station, a handful of students are writing in journals, summarizing books they have read. The students chose one of two books to read and decided as a group how many pages a day they would be responsible for reading. One group thought they could read twenty pages a day, so they could finish in a week. Most of them did; the rest finished over the weekend. "The peer pressure is greater than if I'm after them," Riedl explains.

The teacher herself runs a station called "How Is It Going?" Today, the group is discussing a chapter from a social studies book about colonial times. "I really believe in students learning how to talk and discuss and share insights on readings and responding to other's ideas in a respectful way," she explains. They talk about the relationships between the Native Americans and the early set-tlers and hypothesize about how the introduction of tobacco may have led to slavery.

Riedl uses this station to gauge how the class is working for the students. Because she is very task oriented, she explains, she has to set aside time to let the students voice concerns. Recently, a stu-dent told her that she felt overwhelmed, that there was just too much to do in class. Another student acknowledged that she, too, felt this way at the beginning of the year but that she had found a strategy to conquer it. She writes down everything the class is sup-posed to do during the week, looks at it, and then she decides what to do first, second, and third. "Kids love to hear other kids' solutions to handling the classroom," Riedl says.

Later in the day, the students disperse into math stations. Some go into an adjacent room, where today they watch *Square One*, a TV math show, and answer questions on a worksheet. Another group works with tangrams, Chinese geometric puzzles.

But most of the students spend the time working through problems in the math book. Because it is an individualized math program, one student is working on remainders while another is on least common multiples. Students take pretests and then read a chapter and do problems. Riedl teaches skills that they cannot seem to get on their own. Students move on to the next chapter after they conquer the end-of-chapter test.

Roland Benson, the principal of North Elementary, points out that with this interdisciplinary, project-oriented, individualized approach, Riedl must keep on top of the skill needs of her students. Her program assumes that children bring more to class than what they learned during the last school year. She must determine the areas the students can fly through and pinpoint where they need more extensive instruction. It is not easy, he says, but Riedl seems to make it work. "If you are attuned to the sparkle of eyes, the smiles on faces, and the changes in the channels of energy," he says, "you see that children are getting involved in their learning because they want to be involved."

Parent Debbie Burroughs puts it this way: "She demands of the students, and they end up demanding of themselves. I don't know how she does it."

• • • • • • •

This school within a school has been a successful testing ground for other ideas Riedl intends to use in her charter school, if given the chance. In the past four years, she has given much thought to the design of classroom space, parental involvement, and student assessment.

In 1990, North Elementary, suffering from a space shortage, set aside money to transform an old locker room into a classroom. Riedl saw an opportunity to design a room that would suit her new teaching methods, and she seized it. She found an architectural firm that would donate its services, called a professor at the University of Minnesota who recommended books on designing spaces for children, and recruited a college senior studying interior design to help coordinate colors. Riedl organized a workshop that brought together these people and resources with students, school administrators, and parents.

The group decided to keep the walls that separated the coaches' rooms and the showers from the locker room to cut down on noise when students work in groups. The floors were carpeted, and movable carpeted structures that can be used as both tables or benches were built. Today, the back of the main room looks like a library, with paperback books displayed on shelves and a circular rack and magazines on a flat rack. But a homey touch also prevails: there are two white wicker chairs with quilted pillows, and Riedl's desk is in one corner, with some shelves that give her a little private space without shutting her off from the classroom.

The presence of parents at the classroom-design workshop is in keeping with Riedl's novel approach to parental involvement. Before Riedl reshaped her classroom, she would only contact parents when a student was having problems. She now asks much more of parents, and they get much more in return. All the parents sign a contract agreeing to volunteer in the classroom half an hour each month. Riedl also asks them to attend information meetings, where they are introduced to some of the classroom work stations. This tactic, she says, helps them understand how different the learning environment will be for their children.

Parents say that the firsthand experience in the classroom helps them shake off their old notions of what a productive classroom should look like. Riedl recounts what one parent told the local school board when it was debating whether to designate her program as a bona fide "learning alternative." The parent said, "Listen, I came into Joan's room and I really didn't know what was going on. I was quite upset. But, my boy learned organizational skills. He learned how to be responsible."

Riedl thinks parents learn from spending time in her classroom. But that is not why she wants them to come. The main reason, she says, is a bit more selfish. "To meet students' needs," she says, "I need help." Parents assist in running the stations, special projects, and field trips. And Riedl is convinced that having parents in the classroom sends a good message to the students. "Parents are the single most important people in these kids' lives," she says. "They can have a strong influence in how the students view school."

Every Monday, the students get a homework packet that must be completed by Friday. Parents are asked to check through the packet and sign it each week. That way, they know what their children are learning, they can see for themselves whether their children are mastering the material, and they can encourage them to budget their time well. The homework packet can also act as a reality check for the teacher; Riedl asks the parents to write her a note if they find anything in the packet confusing or misleading.

In her dream school, Riedl would equip each classroom with a phone to make it easier for the teachers to contact parents during the day. She would also have someone take her class for a few days during the year so she could contact her parent volunteers to determine their skills and work out schedules.

Because communicating with parents is so important to Riedl, she is careful to assess her students in ways that the parents will understand. The teacher realizes that most are accustomed to academic progress being measured by tests. So, even though Riedl does not depend on basals to teach reading, she continues to use reading comprehension tests included in the books.

For the same reason, Riedl would continue to use standardized tests to assess students in her charter school, in addition to the more "authentic" evaluations she has developed over the past few years.

Traditional multiple-choice and standardized tests gave Riedl an adequate picture of her students' progress when her teaching was mostly lecture and textbook work. But since students in her redesigned classroom are expected to learn to communicate, organize their own learning, and demonstrate creativity, among other things, Riedl discovered that she needed measurements that more precisely chronicle their work and show their progress and per-formance. Now, students maintain portfolios of writing assign-ments and journals. The classroom video camera also archives the children's progress. A comparison between early tapes of the chil-dren's news summaries and a recent tape, for example, shows that their ability to synthesize and relay information effectively has greatly improved.

Gone, too, are the days when Riedl kept the standards for eval-uation from the students. When making an assignment, Riedl always outlines how they will be evaluated on it. For an oral pre-sentation of a project, for example, Riedl prints out a list of the points she will give them for such things as eye contact, self-pre-sentation, use of visual aids, thoroughness of research, and content.

Riedl also asks students to evaluate themselves. "I want them to be able to say, 'I'm having problems with fractions or decimals. I need help on this,'" she says. She often asks them how they think they did on a project. The payoff comes when students gain the ability to evaluate their own work in order to improve it. Shortly after Christmas break, Riedl collected her students' journals. For the most part, she was pleased with their writing, but she told the class that she had asked a few students to rewrite sections. The surprise came when a student who had done satisfactory work approached her and said, "Mrs. Riedl, I was looking over this, and I was won-dering if I should redo this part." Riedl let the student know that that is what real learning is all about.

• • • • • • •

For the past four years, Riedl has consciously set aside time to familiarize herself with the latest ideas in education. She has put many of her staff in-service days to use reading, attending work-shops, and observing other classrooms. In 1991, she even persuaded her school board to let her take every Friday off, unpaid, to con-tinue these activities.

Riedl attributes much of her professional growth to her relationship with teachers in the Clara Barton Open School in Min-
neapolis and three schools in the Bellevue (Washington) School
District. "I haven't come up with all this on my own," she admits.
"I take bits and pieces of what I know will work for me."

Riedl first read about the Bellevue schools in a software newslet-
ter. Their work reinforced some of what she had been trying in her
class, so she developed a telephone relationship with Marian Peiffer, a teacher at Ardmore Elementary School. Riedl would phone
her and pick her brain about some details of the Bellevue program.
"Do you use desks?" she once asked. Peiffer told her that they use
tables. After talking about it awhile, both agreed that card tables,
which could be folded up and put away, would be ideal.

In fall 1990, Riedl's district paid the airfare for her to visit Bellevue. She spent four days with the teachers there, watching. She
noticed that they let the students work for long blocks of time, an
option she had been wrestling with. "It was a great learning experience to follow other teachers, talk to them, tell them what I'm
doing, and get their feedback," she says.

Riedl has also borrowed ideas from some of the more renowned
minds in education. For example, she has customized some aspects
of Mortimer Adler's paideia proposal in her classroom. "I'm not rigid
Adler, but I like the framework," she says. "It's natural." Adler
believes that teachers have to build students' knowledge base. So,
every Thursday and Friday, Riedl offers something she calls
"Choices," which gives students the opportunity to play games that
expose them to geography, authors, artists, and architecture.

And Riedl has not been afraid to embrace some tried and true
methods. "There are some traditional, old-fashioned ways of teaching that I believe in and put into the curriculum," she says. She thinks
it is important, for example, to teach students how to take notes and
write a business letter, narrative, and descriptive story. Riedl's principal notes that "she doesn't have fear of stepping out of the crowd or of
stepping back into it if she sees that is the right way to go."

• • • • • • •

Riedl's proposal for a charter school is under consideration in both the Princeton and nearby St. Cloud school districts. Her dream school would be shaped around her current teaching methods. At first, the school would serve sixty students, one class of second and third graders and another of fourth and fifth graders. The teachers would keep some of the same students for two years and would work as a team, sharing ideas and designing activities for use in both classrooms. Riedl's primary role would be to teach; she would share the administrative duties with the other teachers. Secretarial and janitorial duties would be shouldered by parents, teachers, and students alike or contracted out. In the second year, Riedl would like to add a sixth and seventh grade classroom.

She believes that the creation of small, alternative public schools like the one she is proposing may be the only way to achieve real change in U.S. education. "You've got to move with the people who can see the vision," she says. "Just like small-group instruction frees you up to do more with different children, change in schools may work better in small pockets."

The past four years have taught Riedl some lessons about the pace and pain of progress. "I have real enthusiasm for change—for getting quality, being cost-efficient, and being a good consumer with tax dollars," she says. "But change is hard in any setting. I know that now."

Riedl did not realize when she started rebuilding her classroom that she was sticking her neck out. She went in thinking she had discovered great new approaches to help kids learn and was surprised when other people did not share her enthusiasm. She even met some resistance when she went to the board to have her program officially designated a school within a school. Now that she is seeking a charter, the naysayers are raising their voices again. Says Bue, one of Riedl's converts, "Anytime you change something so dramatically and especially if tax money is going to support it, it has to be explained many, many times before it can sink in that it will work."

The process has shown Riedl how hard it is to try something different in a society that rewards conformity. "In upsetting the status quo, you take a risk," she says. "When you put forth your ideas, there is always the possibility that they might be ridiculed."

The battle is made tougher, she says, by the poor image many people have of teachers. "Elementary school teachers don't have a lot of status," she explains. "It's easy to believe sometimes that you have no right to speak your mind." Before major meetings, she gets psyched up by telling herself, "Listen, you are fine."

Nowadays, most parents, local educators, and school district officials agree that Riedl's risk taking has earned her the respect of the community. "She has changed her school by what she has done in her classroom," says Benson, Riedl's principal. "She showed others that it is OK to do things differently as long as it better meets the needs of the kids."

Riedl says the leadership role has changed her. "Being out there, breaking new ground, and probing into new territory has made me stronger, more self-confident, more focused, more diplomatic, and more adaptable to working with the system in the decision-making process," she says. "My students are better for it, and I'm better for it."

Elizabeth Schulz

♦ ♦ ♦ ♦ ♦ ♦ ♦

Joan Riedl's charter school proposal was not among those selected for implementation in Minnesota. As of January 1994, she was still teaching her fourth and fifth grade class at North Elementary School and was writing a book about how educational technology can give teachers in heterogeneous classrooms more time for personal, in-depth teaching.

This chapter originally appeared as an article in *Teacher Magazine*, April 1992.

4

$\cdots\cdots\cdots\cdots\cdots\cdots\cdots\cdots\cdots\cdots\cdots$

All About Adam

Adam Urbanski

Adam Urbanski was sitting through a contentious meeting with leaders of the Rochester Teachers Association (RTA) recently when one of them turned to him in anger. "Urbanski," the official said, "if you have your way, the union as we know it will be dead." As Urbanski remembers proudly, "I was supposed to act like a whipped puppy, but I leaned forward and said, 'That's my whole purpose.'"

If Urbanski had his way, teachers' unions as they exist today would be a thing of the past. That would include the 3,500-member RTA, which he has led since 1981. In its place, Urbanski and some of his like-minded colleagues are trying to bring about what he calls "a comfortable marriage between unionism and professionalism." Their new union would be concerned with the welfare not only of its members but also of public education—the union's "industry," as Urbanski calls it—and of children, its "clients."

For the past several years, Urbanski, forty-five, has been a key architect of an innovative effort to rebuild Rochester's troubled schools. His willingness to reconsider time-honored labor practices has brought him national recognition as the leader of a new breed of "nontraditional" union presidents who are viewed as partners, not adversaries, in the crusade to improve schools.

"Not only has Adam been willing to rethink what it means to be a professional teacher in the context of a union," says Linda Darling-Hammond, a professor at Teachers College, Columbia University, who has worked closely with him, "but he has also been incredibly thoughtful and inventive about educational practices in ways that are way ahead of the average local community's thoughts about how schools ought to look and ought to be run."

In Rochester, however, good ideas only go so far. While Urbanski has a national reputation as a bold innovator, critics in his own backyard charge that he has driven up teachers' salaries without delivering the dramatic improvements in student achievement they had expected.

Marvin Jackson, president of the District Parent Council, an umbrella parent and community group, complains, "Reform here in Rochester has been about adults, not kids. It has been about teachers' salaries and the profession of teaching." William Johnson, president of the Urban League of Rochester and a watchful critic of the reform efforts, calls Urbanski "parochial" and says his reputation as a nontraditional leader is overblown. "When the crunch time comes, he is able to forget all of that and to return to the role which he's really elected for," Johnson says, "and that is to protect the interest of his teachers to the exclusion of any other community interests."

The tensions and suspicions inherent in an attempt to radically alter roles and expectations have been heightened by the recession. In the boom-time 1980s, when the district was enjoying double-digit increases in state aid, Rochester teachers' high salaries were generally a source of pride. Now, they have become a lightning rod for criticism and frustration with what some say is the slow pace of improvement in the city's schools.

The complaints have not put Urbanski on the defensive. He says he would be the first to admit that the reforms launched with such fanfare in 1987 have largely failed to produce the sweeping changes they seemed to promise. "The most likely criticism, the most legitimate criticism, would be that reform is needed—just not these specific reforms," he says. "Not only would I not resent such conclusions, I may be leading those who are making those allegations . . . that reform is as necessary as it has always been, but given

what we are learning, these may not be the specific reforms" needed
to bring about the desired improvements.

This winter, the issue of money came to a head. The board of
education and Rochester's brand-new superintendent found themselves facing a multimillion-dollar, midyear budget deficit. District
officials broached the idea of salary concessions with the teachers'
union. In response, Urbanski launched an all-out assault on Rochester's bureaucracy.

For years, he had complained in his characteristically colorful
language about bureaucrats' emphasis on "administrivia" and their
"snoopervision" of teachers. But this time, it was different. Urbanski gained the approval of the union's policy-making Representa-
tive Assembly to buy a full-page advertisement in the local
newspaper listing the job titles and salaries of the district's administrative employees.

Superimposed over the type in bold letters were the words "No
wonder they have a budget problem."

With that tactic, the union leader whose name had become syn-
onymous with cooperative labor-management relations staked out
an unambiguously adversarial position. "I see myself and teachers
locked in a death match with the bureaucracy," Urbanski explains.
"I take this stuff more seriously than they even think. Bureaucracy,
by nature and by definition, is hostile to democratic dynamics, to
reform, and to good pedagogy."

The union's position has antagonized Urbanski's critics, who
believe he has overstepped his bounds. "Adam wants to run the
city school district," complains Jackson of the District Parent
Council. "You won't go anywhere if you get public opinion against
you, and he's standing precariously close to opinion starting to turn
against him."

But Urbanski insists that cutting the bureaucracy is the district's
only hope for both long-term fiscal health and preservation of its
school reform initiatives. "I assume that if they have no choice, they
will retrench themselves," he says, "so we must rob them of any
other choices."

. . . .

It was not supposed to be this way.

In 1987, Urbanski and then-Superintendent Peter McWalters announced they had reached agreement on a new contract that would give teachers handsome raises in exchange for assuming new roles.

Many of the reform plans in the contract were contained in a series of "agreements to agree," with the details to be fleshed out later. There would be planning teams at each school, made up of a majority of teachers, to set goals for the schools and have a voice in deciding who would teach there and who would serve as the principal.

Teachers in the city's middle and high schools would be responsible for groups of about twenty students. The idea of this "home-base" guidance program was to establish a sense of continuity for the city's highly mobile students, which would give them a familiar adult to turn to for advice and counseling. Teachers also were expected to make contact with their students' homes, either through personal visits or telephone calls.

And the city's 2,600 teachers would be arrayed along a four-step career ladder that gave teachers at the top the opportunity to earn substantial bonuses for taking on additional responsibilities. The contract also incorporated the district's existing peer assistance and review program, through which teachers mentored new hires and counseled veteran teachers who were having trouble.

But what captured the headlines were the raises granted to teachers: over the life of the three-year contract, they would see their salaries increase by 40 percent, while lead teachers earning bonuses would be able to make almost $70,000 a year.

Finally, it seemed, a school district was willing to pay teachers professional wages for assuming professional duties. Lead teachers, for example, were to waive their seniority rights and take on the most challenging teaching assignments. All city teachers were to teach more days and work more hours. And seniority would no longer govern all transfers. Instead, they would be contingent upon the approval of a school's planning team.

Urbanski and McWalters quickly became a sought-after duo on the speaking circuit and an example of the cooperative spirit that many experts argued was an essential prerequisite for transforming schools. Both men were quite candid about the failures of the 33,000-student school district. Although comparatively small, Rochester was plagued with the high failure and dropout rates, teen pregnancies, and discipline problems associated with much larger school districts. The challenge was daunting: nearly 70 percent of the district's students were poor and members of minority groups.

No one proved better at deploring the "business as usual" that had produced Rochester's woes than Urbanski. In the Polish accent that still colors his speech, Urbanski lectured teachers, business leaders, community groups—anyone who would listen. Frequently, he turned to the local newspapers and television stations to get his message across. "The problem with schools is not that they are no longer as good as they once were," he loved to say. "The problem is that they are precisely as they always were, but the needs of society and the needs of our students have changed significantly."

For those resistant to change, he argued that "if we always do what we've always done, we will always get what we always got." Therefore, his reasoning went, it was imperative to make fundamental changes in the classroom. He talked endlessly about making learning more real-to-life, changing the way students are grouped and sorted, and redefining teaching to include knowledge of individual students and their needs, not just of a subject. Implicitly, and sometimes explicitly, the union president also criticized teachers. "I see teachers who actually have signs on their doors that say, 'Knowledge dispensed; bring your own container,'" Urbanski once told a Rochester journalist. "This is in spite of the fact that we know that you cannot 'learn' someone. They have to do the learning. We have failed to change. The educational system, including the teachers, has failed to change."

His admirers say Urbanski relished the task of educating the Rochester community about the need for restructuring. "He is a very, very good teacher," says Mary Barnum, a retired high school

English teacher who has known Urbanski for years. "And he's very, very bright."

His message was particularly appealing to talented teachers who felt constrained by traditional notions of schooling. Inspired by Urbanski's leadership, Ester Gliwinski, a highly regarded first grade bilingual teacher, left a job in private sector management to return to Rochester's classrooms. "He has taken the time to think through a philosophy of education," she says of Urbanski. "He knows the direction he wants us to go, and he has a real clear sense of what the school district could be and the classroom could be."

While Urbanski continues to hold fast to his dreams, he is no longer as confident of how to reach them. What the Rochester district created, he says, was "process-fixated, adult-oriented stuff" rather than levers to force change where it matters most—in the city's classrooms. "On bulk," he admits, "it isn't working more than it's working, but I wouldn't have traded it." At least no one can accuse him, he adds, "of living above the clouds or speculating in an ivory tower, because I have to eat what I cook. Sometimes, it doesn't taste very good."

• • • • • • •

Urbanski is a classic American success story: a Polish immigrant who came to the United States in 1960 at the age of fourteen and worked as a shoe-shine boy to make money. "I have always identified with poor kids," he says. "I didn't have to speculate what it's like for a poor child—I was one. I came to this country without enough money to buy things for myself, and schools made a difference for me."

Urbanski was born in Mosciska, Poland, in 1946. When he was eleven, his mother and father, a tailor, decided to leave the Soviet satellite to find the freedom to practice their Catholic faith and the opportunity to make a better life for themselves free of communist control. Posing as Jews, the Urbanskis and their seven sons were permitted to leave Poland. Their departure was the start of a long odyssey through Eastern Europe that finally led the family to Israel, where the Urbanskis lived in a refugee settlement and sold dough-nuts to earn money to pay for their passage to the United States.

During those years, young Adam learned to speak French, Ital-ian, and Hebrew, in addition to his Polish and Russian. His family had been unable to find a sponsor in the United States until Adam, an altar boy, met an American missionary priest who helped the Urbanskis find a sponsor in Rochester.

When they finally arrived in the United States, Urbanski has often recalled, he snuck away from his family and kissed the ground for joy. Eventually becoming accustomed to the strange ways of his new land, Urbanski graduated from high school and went on to earn a bachelor's degree in political science from the University of Rochester in 1969. That year, he began teaching social studies at Rochester's Franklin High School; in 1975, he received a doctorate in American social history from the same university.

Barnum recalls that Urbanski had never served on a citywide union committee when he decided to run for president, although he was the shop steward at his school. His friends convinced him to take the plunge after gathering signatures for him on a petition. What galvanized Urbanski, she says, was a bitter strike in 1980 that resulted in only marginal salary increases and actually cost teachers because they were penalized under state law for every day they stayed out of their classrooms. "He simply could not believe we had such a small increase after a strike," she remembers. "He really is hard-nosed on money items. I've had people tell me he will keep negotiators for days fighting over five bucks. And that's exactly what people expect of him. That's very much a part of him."

Urbanski's belief in unionism runs deep, driven by the convic-tion that collective bargaining offers workers the opportunity to achieve "self-determination." When he assumed the leadership of the RTA in 1981, Urbanski immediately strengthened the union's negotiating position by bringing in financial analysts to comb through the district's budgets. The union's success in delivering good contracts solidified teachers' support for Urbanski and laid the groundwork for expanding negotiations into areas that are not usually contained in teaching contracts.

When people complained that the 1987 teachers' contract would drive up all district employees' salaries, Urbanski remembers, he felt proud. "I called a press conference to plead guilty to a conspiracy to raise the aspirations of workers," he says. "I believe that there can be no parity among unequals. If you don't want me to be a full partner, I will be no partner at all."

Notions of just what constitutes a partnership differ, however. The RTA's recent attack on the district's bureaucracy struck some people who were already wary of the union as a bald power play at a time when the superintendent was new and the school board divided. Among other things, the union proposed negotiating a reduction in the number of administrators to the national teacher-administrator average by July 1992 and to the city's teacher-student ratio by the following summer.

People who are offended by his bureaucrat bashing are not arguing with what he is saying, contends Urbanski, but with the fact that he is saying it. "Let them tell me why the logic of the national average in the administrator-teacher ratio is so bad to propose, so harmful to students," he says. "I am making trouble, but I am not making trouble unwittingly. I believe that there is no real change unless all hell breaks loose. When everything goes smoothly and we're all very polite and cordial with each other, there is really nothing happening."

Despite his fiery rhetoric, in person Urbanski is somewhat formal and reserved. He says he does not socialize much, preferring to spend what little free time he has with his wife, Sunday, and their two children. Union members who have worked closely with Urbanski say he is famous for being stubborn but welcomes their suggestions. He has a self-deprecating sense of humor (he has been known to crack a Polish joke or two about himself) and is considered to be a caring friend. That some quarters of the Rochester community harbor suspicions about his motives is not news to Urbanski. He has heard charges that he wants to use his office as a stepping-stone to a higher position in the American Federation of Teachers, the RTA's national parent organization, or that he is an egotistical media chaser who cannot resist an opportunity to appear on television or be quoted in the newspapers. Both, he says, are false. "Am I in the media because I like to see myself on television?" he asks. "I never watch myself on television. I use it in order to get our point across and to educate the public."

Those who believe he is angling for bigger fish to fry simply misjudge his motives, Urbanski says, adding that he has all the access he could want to national policy makers as a member of the National Board for Professional Teaching Standards and several national advisory boards. His numerous roles take Urbanski away from Rochester so much that Adam Kaufman, the district's lawyer and chief negotiator, fondly refers to him as "our peripatetic Polish president."

"At first, everybody accused me, even teachers, of saying the right things to the right audience, because you're not going to be around very long and you're going to go off and God knows what they had in mind for me," Urbanski says. "They've been saying that for years. Not only am I still in Rochester, but I don't think my worst critics would say that I act like I'm trapped in Rochester."

In the day-to-day Rochester fray, however, Urbanski generally does not answer his detractors. "I don't explain me a lot because I don't think this is about me," he says. "This is not to see how much Urbanski can accomplish. This is to see if, for the first time in the history of the country or maybe the world, we can make schools successful for all children."

◆ ◆ ◆ ◆ ◆ ◆ ◆

In 1990, Urbanski and the union's negotiating team reached an agreement with the school district on a successor to the 1987 contract that they believed would be another bold step toward that goal. That summer, a joint task force had worked with the

National Center on Education and the Economy, a Rochester-based think tank, to hammer out a system for holding teachers, students, parents, administrators, and the larger Rochester community accountable for creating a system that would ensure every child's academic success.

The issue of accountability had been festering in Rochester for years. In a sense, it was created by Urbanski and McWalters, who talked a great deal about holding teachers accountable for student performance. At the time, they viewed the longer hours, school-based planning teams, career ladder, and heightened expectations for "ownership" of students as ways to achieve it. The trouble was that many Rochester taxpayers, footing the bill for the salary increases, either were not convinced that the reforms really would hold teachers' feet to the fire or were disappointed when they did not immediately see a payoff for their investment.

There is a sense now that the first teaching contract was over-sold, says Richard Raymond, a recently retired high school mathematics teacher who was active in the union. "I think the community was sold a bill of goods way back," Raymond says. "People were led to believe with this new contract, everything was going to be OK. I think both sides did that, to a degree."

But Sonia Hernandez, a former analyst at the national center and now the director of education policy for Texas Gov. Ann Richards, says there was always a "tinge of cynicism" about school reform in the city. "There was always an underlying cynicism, just below the surface, within every constituency," she says, "the local government, the central office administrators, the ranks of the teachers, and the parents."

Both negotiating teams heard the continuing drumbeat for teacher accountability as they worked on the new contract. What they devised was an evaluation system that would largely be controlled by teachers and would determine how much of a raise, if any, each teacher would receive. It was another groundbreaking agreement, this time much more specific than the series of "agreements to agree" that had drawn complaints from some teachers.

From the start, however, warning signs arose that this contract would be a much harder sell than the last one. School board members openly discussed the pressure they felt from constituents to hold down salaries as New York State's revenues drained away. Despite their hesitation, board members approved the agreement. For his part, Urbanski promoted the contract as a way to provide "incentives for success and disincentives for failure that are sorely lacking in our system."

Rochester's teachers turned it down by seventy-five votes, with nearly a thousand members sitting out the election all together. The rejection of the contract was a stunning blow to Urbanski, who was widely regarded as one of the union's most popular presidents and had never been in serious jeopardy of losing his post. He considered resigning. He also declared the issue of pay for performance to be "dead," noting that it was "one way to represent accountability, but not the only way."

"I was standing right behind him when the ballots were counted, right in front of the TV cameras, and I thought his body was going to sink right into the floor," says Barnum, the retired teacher. "It was a terrible shock to him. I don't think he ever dreamed the damn thing would go down. I have never seen a human being who looked so alone."

Rochester residents who were dead set on seeing teachers' pay tied to their job performance insist that the message sent that day by his troops has changed Urbanski, forcing him back into a more traditional role to mollify his members. "From that point forward," says Michael Fernandez, an Eastman Kodak employee and the school board's most vocal proponent of a pay-for-performance system, "the debate and the focus began to change, and a lot of the discussion from Adam and his leadership seemed to develop in more traditional ways."

That view is shared even by some of Urbanski's admirers, including Gliwinski. "I just know there's been a real difference that I feel very badly about," she says. "Adam is a paradox in so many ways. He's absolutely a man you would write a Greek tragedy about. I've seen him when he's had tremendous success, and I've seen him in meetings when he's being unfairly and viciously attacked by people in teaching for what I think are the wrong reasons. I've seen him laughed off the stage, and he doesn't leave."

Accusations that he has backed away from bold leadership to retain the support of the city's teachers are "simply not true," Urbanski says. "They elected me to lead, and I lead. I try to in a way that is sensitive to their realities and a good match with either what they would support or what they are capable of, even if they're not ready for it right now."

The fact that few states or school districts in the nation have been able to devise successful programs to tie teachers' pay to their job performance does not seem to hold much sway with proponents of such a scheme for Rochester. Urbanski says he was willing to venture down that path because "there is absolutely no question in my mind that there should be some relationship between the work that teachers do and the remuneration of teachers. I just don't know yet what it is. . . . I showed an honest willingness to explore the issues thoughtfully and sincerely and honestly and straightforwardly."

The September 1990 vote began a long and sometimes bitter year of wrangling that finally yielded a contract acceptable to both sides in April. During that year, to force progress on the contract talks, some teachers stopped participating in their school planning teams. Urbanski himself refused to attend meetings of a districtwide committee on school-based planning. In fact, he refused to set foot in the central office until teachers got a settlement.

These traditional job actions upset some parents and underscored doubts in the minds of residents who had questioned rank-and-file teachers' commitment to reforms. "Adam is a strategist," observes former superintendent McWalters, who is now the Rhode Island commissioner of education. "He will do what he needs to do to win the battle.

"What we were trying to do, we've always known, puts labor and management in a very precarious position," he adds, "because you're trying to work cooperatively in an institutional structure that expects you to be adversaries." Whenever he found himself in a public battle with Urbanski, McWalters says, he wrote off the incidents as examples of times when it was necessary for each side to play a role. Administrators who watched Urbanski dominate the news, the former superintendent remembers, criticized him for letting the union leader get the upper hand. But McWalters says he always trusted the "substance" that was driving Urbanski, knowing they sought the same ends through different means. "He's still the best," McWalters says. "I would rather go down fighting with him than anyone else."

Others who have jousted with Urbanski are less charitable. Hans DeBruyn, a Xerox employee and parent who sits on the district's negotiating team, and Urbanski had a falling-out when DeBruyn tried to send a parent survey home with children during negotiations. Urbanski asked teachers not to let their students act as couriers, arguing that it was inappropriate. DeBruyn charges that this winter, during hearings on budget cuts, teachers urged their students to bring their parents to the meetings to argue against cutting teaching jobs. He says Urbanski did nothing to stop the practice; Urbanski says if teachers behaved that way, it was on their own and the union has a standing policy against using students in such a manner.

In a time when there is general agreement that school reform cannot succeed without the involvement of parents and the community at large, Urbanski seems unconcerned about alienating the district's organized parent representatives. He says he is aware that he is viewed as not wanting parents to be involved in schools. "You see," he explains, "I don't pander to them. I try not to pander to anybody. The fact that I don't treat them with the same patronizing tones that some bureaucrats do, they don't like it. But I'm not out to please them. I'm out to educate their kids better."

The bottom line for the union president is the mantra he coined in the mid 1980s. At that time, the district's administrators filed a lawsuit against some aspects of the new peer review program. Urbanski decided then that bringing about fundamental changes in schools was more important than reaching unanimity on each point. Reforms, he says, must proceed "with them if we can and without them if we must."

Resisting the pressure to create a merit-pay system, he says, takes more courage than giving the public what it wants. "Just like it takes more courage not to give them higher test scores than to give [them], because we could give them higher-scoring dummies. We could stop teaching and start drilling for the tests. Stooping to satisfy the worst impulses of people or the conventional wisdom, if you want an oxymoron, is not necessarily responsible behavior."

• • • • • • •

What is responsible behavior now, given the lessons that have been learned by teachers in Rochester? Urbanski and some of his members say they fear the district has created a new kind of bureaucracy with its school planning teams and various teaching positions removed from the classroom. "I feel like I have entered into a partnership with a system that by nature is incapable of paving the way for real reform and real change," Urbanski says. "I may have to propose to teachers that we engage in a full-scale campaign of reform without permission, of pedagogical mass insubordination."

School-based planning, for example, has "democratized" the schools but has also "tied teachers up in knots," he says. "Even teachers in schools where it's working are saying, 'Look at the price we have to pay for it. Endless meetings, time away from teaching— Adam, I'm not sure if the cure is not worse than the disease.'" The time might be worthwhile if the process had penetrated the classroom, Urbanski says, but too often it has not. "In some instances it managed to improve the level of comfort among adults, but you'd be hard-pressed to notice any difference with kids," he notes.

Part of the problem was with the name, he says, which implied that schools would be run by committees. Urbanski says he would now like to call the groups "instructional design teams" and leave the day-to-day "administrivia" of school life to the principal. What if, he continues, the instructional design team or the faculty had the right to evaluate the principal annually and decide whether to retain or oust him or her? That lever would permit teachers to assume that their work would be supported, he says.

As for the perennial issue of teacher evaluations and compensation, he adds, why not create a local board for professional teaching standards, modeled after the national group, to determine what teachers should know and be able to do and to certify them? "And maybe, just maybe, only those who get such board certification should get any raises whatsoever," he suggests.

"I think about these things increasingly hard," Urbanski says. "This is not something I am getting tired of explaining. I feel like I am just on the verge of understanding what the dynamics are and what the processes are. I'm learning."

His only regret, he says, is the time he has spent away from his family. His son, Mark, is now twenty-one, while his daughter Lisa is nineteen. "Eleven years ago, I should have been smart enough not to run for this job," he says. "With kids, there is no such thing as quality time; there is just time. There's no way I could have done this job and not paid the price."

But he has loved every minute of it. "Especially when we didn't know what we would do a half-hour later," he remembers. "Especially when we were going for all the marbles—when we could lose it all or gain it all. And especially when we shocked the hell out of everybody, because nobody had ever done this before."

Ann Bradley

* * * * * * *

Adam Urbanski was reelected in 1993 to his seventh term as president of the Rochester Teachers Association. He plans to run again in 1995.

Dave Schlabowske

This chapter originally appeared as an article in *Teacher Magazine*, August 1992.

5

Dynamic Duo
Bob Peterson and Rita Tenorio

I t is a late winter day in Milwaukee, and a brilliant sun has elevated the temperature to a balmy fifty degrees—a rarity for these
climes. All along Lake Drive, the road that hugs the Lake Michigan shoreline, people are bicycling, tossing Frisbees, walking, and
celebrating the golden weather. But holed up inside a two-story red
brick building several miles from the lake, a dozen men and women
resist the promise of spring and concentrate on the task at hand.
They are volunteers, dressed in the casual uniform of the day—
jeans, flannel shirts, sweatshirts, and sneakers. Some wear buttons
touting a particular cause. A three-month-old boy naps cozily atop
a Formica conference table while his mother works. In these
cramped quarters, haphazardly decorated with mismatched furniture, posters, and plants suspended in macrame hangers, they pass
the afternoon proofreading copy, writing, and typing corrections
into a computer.

Were it two decades ago, this could easily be a conclave of
antiwar activists. Despite the wrinkles and graying hair, these men
and women are clearly agitators. But unlike their counterparts
from the 1960s, the people gathered here are not outsiders. They
agitate within the system. Their cause: to reform the Milwaukee
public schools. They are the editors and publishers of a first-of-its-
kind newspaper, a periodical produced by an independent group
of educators. Collectively, they spend hundreds of hours each

month getting out their message of reform to colleagues and the community at large.

Two among them, Bob Peterson and Rita Tenorio, exemplify the passion and energy that has driven *Rethinking Schools* since the quarterly tabloid was started six years ago.

Peterson and Tenorio have been at the forefront of school reform in Milwaukee for nearly a decade. They cofounded *Rethinking Schools* in 1986 and a year later helped establish a nationwide organization for educators and parents seeking to change public education. Then in 1988, the two helped create the experimental Fratney Street School, where they are putting the principles and ideas they preach into practice. And last year, they headed a reform slate that gained control of the local teachers' union.

Says Anita Simansky, a volunteer proofreader for *Rethinking Schools* and a guidance counselor in the nearby Kenosha public school system, "These are people who, when they were very young, decided on a lifetime conviction of putting a lot of time and energy into trying to change the world."

* * * * * * *

People who have known Peterson for a long time say it is only natural that he grew up to be some sort of reformer. That he did so as a schoolteacher is another matter entirely.

Peterson was raised in Madison, Wisconsin, in the late 1960s and early 1970s when it was the heartland's hotbed of student activism. At Madison West High School, he worked for student rights and against the Vietnam War. Peterson thought of high school itself as an infringement of his rights, and he rebelled by participating in sit-ins and walkouts over the dress code and other issues. "For the most part," he says, "I really despised school."

Nonetheless, after high school, Peterson took a job as a teacher's aide in Milwaukee. His first day on the job did little to improve his opinion of public schools. It happened to coincide with the first day of busing to desegregate the school system. Black students were being bused to his predominantly white high school. The bus arrived late, and as the wary students emerged, a physical education teacher stood at the school door noisily demanding that they go get tardy slips. "I couldn't believe it," Peterson says. "Here are these kids, they're scared, and this gym teacher is yelling at them."

Surprising even himself, Peterson subsequently enrolled in the University of Wisconsin, Milwaukee, got a degree, and began teaching in a city school in 1980.

Like Peterson, Rita Tenorio had not set her sights on a career in teaching while growing up in the Milwaukee suburbs. But as a young woman coming of age on the verge of the women's movement, it was one of three career options suggested by her high school counselors. "They told me I could be a teacher, a social worker, or a nurse," she recalls. She chose social work. But during her field experience at the University of Wisconsin, Milwaukee, she discovered how much she enjoyed children. So, Tenorio switched majors and in the early 1970s, took her first full-time teaching job at an all-black, inner-city parochial school.

She liked the work. Her students' parents had high expectations for them and were actively involved in their education. But the pay was bad; after eight years at the school, she was only making $8,000 a year. To gain some financial security and to get involved in a new bilingual education program, Tenorio decided to move to the public schools.

The switch, however, was not all positive. She was surprised to find that parental expectations and involvement in her new school were both disappointingly low. And she was soon disenchanted with the curriculum and pedagogy the district imposed. At the parochial school, she had been free to use components of what is now known as the whole-language approach to instruction. But not at her new public school. It seemed that each year, the district added another basal reader to the curriculum. "I really resisted having to do some of the things public schools said we had to do," says Tenorio, whose principal gave her some leeway. "At times, it really did feel like I was a subversive. If there was a choice between painting on an easel or [completing] two workbook pages, in my mind there was no choice."

Peterson and Tenorio met in 1980 at a meeting of the city's human relations committee and quickly realized they shared many of the same educational philosophies and concerns, including an unhappiness with the city's public school system. "We sort of connected at that point," Tenorio says. Strengthened by their mini-alliance, both plunged into more civic and school activities.

In the mid 1980s, Tenorio and Peterson began meeting regularly with a group of educators who shared their frustrations—with both the school system and the lack of leadership in the teachers' union. The Milwaukee school district was plagued with all the problems of major urban districts: rampant truancy, a severe dropout problem, declining test scores, low grade-point averages, and a growing minority enrollment coupled with a lack of minority teachers. The central office and the school board were formulating reform plans but without much input from teachers or their union.

Peterson, Tenorio, and their colleagues decided they needed to find a way to stir up the waters and get more people involved—some sort of sustained way to promote their ideas. So, the idea for *Rethinking Schools* was born.

As one member of the group would later describe it, "*Rethinking Schools* is the child of our frustration with how little voice teachers are allowed in the debates over what is and what should be happening in the schools. In Milwaukee, as elsewhere, the public schools are in deep trouble. But most of the people authoritatively offering solutions to the public have been central office officials, legislators, and businessmen. When the blue ribbon commissions are established to investigate the schools and offer reforms, they usually include only one or two classroom teachers, often invited as an afterthought. As pawns rather than respected colleagues in the search for school reform, teachers often feel isolated and powerless."

The newspaper was created to end the isolation and impotence and make teachers central players in reform. "We no longer wanted to be on the defensive all the time on school issues," says Peterson. "We wanted to have a vehicle in which we could begin to address in a proactive way issues that affect teachers and parents."

The first idea was to produce something like an academic journal. But that idea soon gave way to a newspaper format, which seemed more appropriate for their mission and more accessible to teachers and the community. Moreover, the availability of desktop publishing software would enable them to do much of the work themselves.

Once a format was established, the group developed a statement of purpose, which still appears in essentially its original form in every issue under the headline "Who We Are." The educators vigorously debated whether their publication would incorporate a cross section of viewpoints or speak with one voice. In the end, they decided that unity would be more powerful.

They chose not to shy away from confrontation. Tenorio's "Confessions of a Kindergarten Teacher," the lead article in the first issue, set the rebellious tone for the publication. In it, she revealed her pedagogical transgression, forsaking the basal reader.

* * * * * * *

In the early days, the editors did not know whether *Rethinking Schools* would survive. When the newspaper first went to press in the 1986–87 school year, the group did not even have enough money to pay the printer. What little they had was scrounged up from house parties, donations, and $10 voluntary subscriptions.

When most of the writing was completed for each issue, the educators, who had but a fleeting knowledge of journalism and the production process, would set up shop in one of the editors' apartments.

David Levine, a former Milwaukee teacher and a member of the original group, recalls one of the early deadline periods: "For the next four days, my small Milwaukee flat would cease being a home in any normal sense of the word. Every flat surface—kitchen table, study desk, borrowed card table—was covered with layout paper. Extra lamps had been imported to augment my dim lighting, and an ugly brown filing cabinet had displaced my living room rocking chair. I would have no place to cook dinner, no privacy, and little rest. I was entering a temporary throwback to my early days of political activism, when we cheerfully let the greater cause jostle and shove personal life into the corner."

The lack of money and amenities were not the only obstacles. Initially, the teachers were also concerned about repercussions from administrators who might take umbrage at the hard-edged copy. After the second issue was published, Peterson was summoned to his principal's office. Although personally supportive of the endeavor, the principal warned him to be cautious. As Peterson recalls, the principal said, "It's like the McCarthy era down at central office. Just tell your people to be very careful."

But nothing untoward occurred. In fact, a member of the original group, Cynthia Ellwood, was later moved, under a new district administration, into the central office as coordinator of a K–12 curriculum reform project. She subsequently became the school system's curriculum director, resigning from the newspaper's staff to avoid any potential conflict of interest.

Many who know the teachers doubt that political repercussions would have quieted them anyway. Says Erin Krause, a newspaper volunteer who teaches with Tenorio and Peterson, "They aren't afraid to step on people's toes."

Nothing was immune from scrutiny. Even the Milwaukee Teachers' Education Association (MTEA) became the target of their criticism, which produced cries of alarm from within the union. According to Tenorio, many union officials were convinced that *Rethinking Schools* had been created as a vehicle to attack and undermine the MTEA. Some union members, Peterson says, even thought the newspaper was being underwritten by another union.

Undermining MTEA "certainly was not the purpose," Tenorio says. But, she adds, the publication was created to challenge every teacher in the school system, including the union leadership. "We can no longer run the union as we have in the past twenty-five years," she says.

In 1989, the teacher-editors' financial plight was eased temporarily thanks to the first of several small grants from the New
World Foundation of New York City. According to Ann Bastian, a
senior program officer at the foundation, "We became interested in
Rethinking Schools not only because of the quality but also because
we thought the paper provided a forum in a way that teachers could
really connect to the community. Rethinking Schools was very crucial in getting teachers actively and independently thinking about
school change themselves." And because the ideas were not being
generated from outsiders, she adds, teachers "were not stuck in a
defensive position and could help set the agenda, which they
should be doing."

The content of Rethinking Schools focuses on many of the crucial
issues facing urban educators and parents today, as well as societal
issues and teaching methods; the editors pay particular attention to
multicultural issues. The paper has run in-depth articles about tracking, whole language, school choice, standardized testing, and
teacher evaluation, among other topics. The front page of the
March/April 1992 issue offers "The Illusion of Choice" and "Examining Proposals for Improving [Milwaukee's Public Schools]: Reform
vs. Scapegoating." Inside stories include "Teachers Evaluating
Teachers," "Recession Goes to the Head of the Class," and "Experimenting with Assessment."

Most of the articles are written by the core group of editors,
although a small stable of correspondents from school systems elsewhere in the country also contribute stories. The writing style is a
blend of reportage, analysis, and advocacy. It is the rare article that
leaves the reader wondering on what side of the issue the writer
falls. The editors have a number of firmly held opinions. They
oppose, for example, choice and the creation of so-called "charter
schools." And they are critical of standardized testing.

The newspaper also excerpts articles and books by prominent
education writers and researchers such as Jonathan Kozol and Linda
Darling-Hammond, a professor of education at Teachers College,
Columbia University. Parents and politicians occasionally contribute

articles to *Rethinking Schools* as well. The back page is reserved for the art, prose, and poetry of schoolchildren.

Linda Christensen, a high school teacher in Portland, Oregon, is one of the regular contributors. "The thing that I really find exciting about *Rethinking Schools* is that it is a collection of teachers who are putting it together," Christensen says. "Most publications that I've seen are specific toward a content area or issues in education. But *Rethinking Schools* really combines all of those. It's about classroom practice but also about the large issues and struggles in education. And it comes from a perspective that is both pro-teacher and pro-student and, at the same time, pro-parent and pro-community."

The paper has grown from a six thousand–circulation periodical to one nearing forty thousand, with an audience as far flung as New Jersey, Kentucky, and California. While the publication is free to Milwaukee teachers, it also has two thousand paid subscribers, most from outside the metropolitan area. This latter group includes a number of teacher educators who use the newspaper in their classrooms. After seeing an issue for the first time, Joyce Penfield, an associate professor of education at Rutgers University, ordered back issues for her students. "It raises very important topics," says Penfield, noting that it tends to be ahead of most other educational journals. "It's very applicable to what I see is good teaching, good learning, and good education."

Even though its annual budget has nearly doubled over the past few years to about $64,000, the paper is by no means a flush operation. Its founders have been able to raise enough money to hire two part-time employees, including a managing editor, and rent modest office space, but it still is mainly produced by volunteers. Dozens show up to unload the printed copies and sort them for distribution to schools, churches, libraries, and other area locales.

The editors have published a few advertisements but generally eschew them because of the potential conflict between the ads and the paper's rebellious philosophy. They also acknowledge that this same philosophy has hindered efforts to score additional foundation support. Consequently, they are putting their energies into expanding the paid subscriber list to six thousand. And the publishers have launched a fundraising campaign, asking readers to make an annual pledge to the publication.

* * * * * * *

As the quincentenary of Columbus's voyage to America approached, the editors of *Rethinking Schools* began to devote considerable space to the explorer. As Peterson puts it, they wanted to provide an "alternative voice" to all the heroic depictions of Columbus that would be forthcoming.

The Columbus articles were so well received that the editors decided to repackage them, along with several other pieces on the topic, into a ninety-five-page booklet titled *Rethinking Columbus*. It turned out to be a big success. First published in September 1991, the booklet is now in its fifth printing and has sold more than 165,000 copies. Orders have come from all parts of the United States and Canada, as well as such exotic locales as Belize and Japan. The Atlanta school system alone purchased five thousand copies.

The success of *Rethinking Columbus* was a blessing, but it also posed some problems. For example, the office workload increased dramatically. Even today, about two-thirds of the thirty to eighty pieces of mail the newspaper receives daily is related to the Columbus booklet. Realizing that they could no longer handle the volume of mail along with all the other demands, the teacher-editors hired Barbara Miner, a parent and former reporter for the *Milwaukee Journal*, as a part-time managing editor.

Says Peterson, "*Rethinking Columbus* propelled us onto the national scene," albeit reluctantly.

To help the newspaper broaden its outlook as its national audience widens, the editors recently established a national advisory board. Their hope is that it will help critique the newspaper, identify prospective writers with differing perspectives, and raise funds.

Although the focus of *Rethinking Schools* has been on Milwaukee, its tone and message clearly have struck a chord with teachers elsewhere. Christina Brinkley, a member of the advisory board, says the paper has had a serendipitous effect. About three years ago, letters started arriving from grateful teachers relieved to learn that they were not alone in their attempts to improve their schools. "The letters were almost heart wrenching," says Brinkley, an associate professor of sociology and women's studies at Bates College in Maine. Until they started reading the newspaper, she says, "those lone teachers had been isolated."

Christensen of Portland adds, *"Rethinking Schools* enables us to look at our local issues in terms of a national picture."

Another project that grew out of *Rethinking Schools* has also contributed to the paper's growing national prominence. Five years ago, Peterson and Tenorio and a number of fellow teachers and parents who advocate activism as an instrument for changing public schools began holding informal meetings. As the group grew, so did its reputation; people from other parts of the country began calling. Things snowballed, and in 1991 the National Coalition of Education Activists officially came into being with five hundred dues-paying members.

The coalition, which Peterson cochairs, serves as a clearinghouse and resource center for parents and teachers. It also sponsors forums in different parts of the country and hosts an annual summer conference. This year's theme is "Breaking Barriers: Schools and Social Justice in Our Communities."

· · · · · · ·

Despite its growing readership and sphere of influence, *Rethinking Schools'* emphasis is still largely on Milwaukee. "We pick articles that we think are going to move things ahead," Peterson says. If the overall perspective shifts to a national audience, Peterson and Tenorio fear the newspaper will become abstract.

In addition, many articles have a hometown political flavor that might be lost if the emphasis shifts. This past spring, for example, the paper ran a piece knocking various community and school leaders—school board members, the mayor, a mayoral aide, and a local radio and television station—for taking whacks at the schools. "Criticizing [Milwaukee public schools, or MPS] is not the problem; this newspaper has never been shy about criticizing MPS," Peterson wrote. "What is disturbing is the lack of analysis behind many of the current criticisms and the potential dangers in several of the proposed 'solutions.'"

The periodical's Milwaukee focus has made it a must read for local policy makers. Even those who are the occasional targets of criticism appreciate the paper's overall high quality. "The publication is well written; its thinking is supported by background data, interviews, good writing," says Milwaukee Mayor John Norquist. "It's really an important part of Milwaukee's political culture now."

The paper's main flaw, he says, is that it is too much a part of the establishment. "Their reform is within the system; they don't threaten the basic premise of the system," he says, citing the newspaper's opposition to parental choice. "If we are going to keep the basic system we have, then *Rethinking Schools* has all kinds of great ideas."

Martin Haberman, a professor of education at the University of Wisconsin, Milwaukee, also credits *Rethinking Schools* for coming up with imaginative and creative ideas. But Haberman, whose research focuses largely on urban education, doubts that the newspaper has accomplished much within the Milwaukee public schools. "I wouldn't credit them with changing anything," he says. "They're nice liberal people. They're good people, hard working, trying to deal with the issues of the day."

Haberman fears that the publication is not reaching the appropriate audience. "The liberals that they appeal to all live in the suburbs," he says. Haberman says he wishes he had the money to make sure that all the parents in the city received copies. And, he adds,

"I wish the school board directors and the budget people and the state legislators read it."

Because they want to be taken seriously by everyone from fellow teachers to inner-city parents and state lawmakers, the editors take great pains to produce a top-notch product. They reject roughly two-thirds of the articles submitted by outside writers. But they are equally tough, if not tougher, on their own work. They spiked their premier edition, slated for mid 1986 publication, because it did not meet the standards they had set for themselves.

The editorial rigor, of course, has meant lots of work and long hours for the teachers involved. Hiring Miner as managing editor has given the teacher-editors a little extra time to carry out their ever-increasing responsibilities.

Peterson's and Tenorio's schedules are particularly dizzying. They both generally arrive at school at about 7:15 A.M. and put in a full day there. After school, they attend union, newspaper, or district committee meetings about four days a week. And then there are the night meetings. Tenorio says she often does not get home until after 9:30 P.M.

Weekends, too, are frequently taken up with business. On one Saturday, for example, Tenorio spent the entire day in union meetings while Peterson revised several newspaper stories. They both worked on the newspaper on Sunday from 1:00 in the afternoon until 9:30 that night, and then they had to get up bright and early the next morning for a 6:30 meeting.

Their growing celebrity has also made them hot commodities on the conference circuit. This is particularly true for Tenorio, who last year was named Wisconsin Teacher of the Year. One friend marvels that Tenorio is able to attend "thirty meetings a day but still knows somehow about Bart Simpson or a [news] report."

Paulette Copeland, an elementary reading teacher who contributes time to *Rethinking Schools*, remarks, "I don't really think anyone would be willing to put in the time they are willing to put in."

But Peterson and Tenorio, neither of whom is married, insist that the long hours and the wrangling are necessary if they are to fulfill their mission. A quick glance at some of their recent accomplishments shows that their efforts are not for naught. A series the paper ran helped persuade former Milwaukee Superintendent Robert Peterkin to spend $100,000 that had been earmarked for basal textbooks on other materials instead. Articles convinced the district to form a council to help schools adopt the whole-language approach. And the publication played a role in swaying the school board to block an outcome-based education approach and a consultant's student assignment plan. The district's assessment task force, which Peterson cochairs, successfully persuaded the district to replace a third grade standardized test with a fourth grade holistic assessment—a move *Rethinking Schools* had advocated.

Says Mary Bills, a district school board member and former chair of the board's curriculum committee, "Many of [the newspaper's] board members were instrumental in helping us change our curriculum. They showed the same dedication to developing our curriculum process as they do to putting out a very timely and useful publication. I'm generally very supportive of the role they play. They make us think, they occasionally make us change what we do, and they bring something to the table."

Tenorio and Peterson attribute their successes to hard work, a proven track record in the classroom, and a tested political strategy. "We have been able to criticize and take issue with policy, but at the same time we have been willing to get involved in the traditional mode of things," Tenorio says.

• • • • • • •

Between meetings on a cool Sunday evening, Tenorio and Peterson stop at a neighborhood restaurant to grab a quick bite to eat. A young woman, a Native American college student majoring in journalism, approaches their table. A dinner companion has pointed them out to her, and she wants to tell them how much she appreciates the wonderful job they are doing. Please let her know, she says, if she can help in any way.

No, they quip, it was not a put-up job for the benefit of the reporter traipsing around with them. But they are obviously pleased, not so much because of the compliment but because they have a potential new recruit who seems to possess many of the qualities they look for to get the job done.

First and foremost these days, that job is their work at Fratney Street School. "In *Rethinking Schools,* we try to offer a vision of what we think should take place in public schools," Tenorio says. "We always try to provide a model. At Fratney, we're trying to take the best of that vision."

Located five blocks from the newspaper's headquarters, Fratney bears the distinct character of a yesteryear neighborhood schoolhouse. Standing four stories tall, the two-tone brown school sits in the middle of a large paved block enclosed by metal fencing.

When Peterson learned that the district planned to close the eighty-year-old structure, he saw an opportunity. He called Tenorio and suggested that they marshal their resources and try to convince the school board not to shut the school but hand it over to them. As Tenorio remembers it, she replied, "OK, we'll work on it." But then, she recalls, "he told me we had to be ready to go by the next week. I said, 'You're crazy.'"

What made Fratney particularly appealing as a site for their experimental school was that it is located in Riverwest, one of the few racially and ethnically mixed communities in Milwaukee. In recent years, this neighborhood of modest bungalows and industry has become home to a socioeconomic brew of blue-collar workers, artists, and professionals.

Tenorio and Peterson quickly organized neighborhood parents and community leaders and launched a successful campaign to persuade the school board to keep Fratney open and let a new staff try a new approach to teaching and learning. "We won," Peterson says. "We were flabbergasted; all of a sudden we were in charge of a school."

But the euphoria was premature. True, the school board had given them the go ahead, but the central office dragged its feet. District administrators, as it turned out, had their own plan for the school. It was not until the district administration changed a short time later and Peterkin became superintendent that Peterson, Tenorio, and their colleagues were given the free reign and support they had sought.

Describing the school's current mission is akin to executing a tongue twister: Fratney is an English-Spanish bilingual, whole-language, site-based-managed, neighborhood specialty school.

* * * * * * *

It is now Monday morning, and Tenorio and her kindergartners—equipped with paper, pencils, and clipboards—stroll around the schoolyard writing down observations for their lesson. A mixture of white, black, and Hispanic children, the class heads back inside the bright, cheery school and down its wide halls and glossy wooden floors.

Then Tenorio, poised with a marker over a piece of newsprint, asks the children, seated in a circle on the floor, what they saw on this *"el lunes, el dos, marzo."*

Hands shoot up and wave. Birds, the school, the ground, telephone lines, *un carro, un palo.* Even though they are in their first year of exposure to the different languages, the English-speaking youngsters appear to comprehend their Spanish-speaking classmates and vice versa.

Two floors below, Peterson is playing host to a group of visiting teachers from Chicago. Explaining Fratney's bilingual approach, he tells them that the teachers at the school build on a child's native language and then help them transfer those skills to the other language.

"The test of our success," he tells one of the visitors, "would be our ability to reach the kids who aren't succeeding."

Peterson is in the parents' resource room, where members of the community are welcome all day long. A paid coordinator works full time to ensure parental and community involvement. Children come in and pepper "Bob" with all sorts of questions. Addressing teachers by their first names, a verboten practice in most schools, is the norm here among students and parents. It is one small way the staff makes parents feel on equal footing with the teachers.

At Fratney, Peterson is officially known as the program implementer. But essentially he is a jack-of-all-trades: the photocopier repairman, recess coordinator, curriculum planner, and teacher. He teaches small reading groups and writing workshops and team-teaches social studies.

Because the program at Fratney is only in its fourth year, the school's faculty and district officials are reluctant to talk in terms of success or failure. An accurate assessment, they say, may be possible in another year or two.

Tenorio's assessment, so far, is mixed. On the positive side, she says, is the nurturing school climate. On the negative, "Kids still come to school with problems that inner-city kids have," she says, and some Anglo students see no reason to learn Spanish. "School climate may be the most important thing for some kids," she adds, "[but] you can't be satisfied that because they're happy to be at school that is enough."

Parent Catherine Liptack had planned to teach her two sons at home until she visited Fratney and learned about the program. "I think the atmosphere is very open and very caring," she says. "There is a real sense that everyone is looking out for each other." Overall, Liptack says she is pleased with her second grader's progress, but she worries about class size. "Even in this program," she laments, "there are too many kids."

As for Tenorio and Peterson, Liptack says, "They're both whirlwinds. Rita is a vivacious, full-of-energy person who is always moving. She is dynamic. Bob is more low-key, but he has a real strong behind-the-scenes leadership style. I think he basically runs the school. He has a way of making things work and keeping things going. He can do five things at once and still be nice to everybody."

• • • • • • •

Peterson and Tenorio's juggling act also includes the MTEA, the largest unaffiliated local teachers' union in the country. Both were elected to the executive board five years ago but, according to Peterson, represented such a minority voice that they were virtually ineffective.

In 1991, however, the two of them ran as part of a reform slate, and a majority of the progressive candidates were elected; Tenorio was elected vice president and Peterson was reelected to the union's executive board.

Mayor Norquist believes the new leadership from *Rethinking Schools* has an opportunity to open up the union to fresh ideas. "The previous [leaders] felt threatened by their own elections," he says. "You had a lot of sclerosis of the arteries."

Says Peterson, "I want our union to be an advocate, not a barrier, to reform." He notes that there are already signs of progress: the MTEA is promoting a mentor program and supporting curriculum reform.

But Tenorio says the election has not eliminated tensions within the MTEA. Tenorio, for example, wants the union to retreat from its traditional adversarial approach to doing business, a stance that some within the organization argue is the equivalent to "giving away the store." That assertion, she says, is untrue. "I am an advocate of teachers," she declares. "I think we have to look at new ways of interacting."

As a result of all their labor, Tenorio and Peterson have come to be seen by many as the leaders of school reform in Milwaukee. But Christensen describes them another way. "*Organizers* would be the term that I would use," she says. "They are really trying to organize the community around the school people in a way that is not around cookies and teas."

Tenorio agrees that organizer is the more accurate assessment. One of their main goals, she says, is to involve others in school reform. "Every person working on a small piece can accomplish something," she says. She points to Erin Krause, who volunteers for each issue of *Rethinking Schools* despite having a young child and a full-time job. "That is a big sacrifice for her," she says.

Besides, Tenorio declares, "I'm not going to be able to continue at this pace forever. There are days when I want it to all go away." She pauses for a moment, and then adds, almost as an afterthought, "I'm a driven person; I need to be challenged all the time."

Both Tenorio and Peterson have been urged to turn their leadership and organizational talents to a principalship or some other administrative post. But they believe the only people who can really turn schools around are teachers—working primarily through the union. "We can't do that once we become part of the administration," Peterson says. "Plus," he adds, a grin spreading across his face, "we love to teach."

Karen Diegmueller

◆ ◆ ◆ ◆ ◆ ◆ ◆

Bob Peterson and Rita Tenorio were not reelected to their leadership positions within the Milwaukee Teachers' Education Association, but they continue to stir up the education establishment through Rethinking Schools. *The Fratney Street School, where both still work, is thriving.*

Fred Mertz

This chapter originally appeared as an article in *Teacher Magazine*, October 1992.

. . . .

6

Personal Best

Charles Vidal

Charles Vidal grabs a handful of new pencils from his desk drawer and heads out of his office into the central courtyard of Evelyn A. Hanshaw Middle School in Modesto, California, where seventh and eighth graders are milling around before the start of school.

He passes three Hispanic boys, all dressed in T-shirts bearing different messages. "Hey, Fresno State," Vidal says to the one wearing a shirt from California State University, Fresno, "come over here." Handing the boy a pencil, Vidal tells him, "Good job. I like your shirt."

The boys continue on their way. But after a couple steps, the other two stop and turn toward Vidal. "Mr. Vidal," both of them say in the nearly unintelligible mumble of thirteen-year-olds talking to adults, "I'm being my personal best."

"Glad to hear it," Vidal responds and passes them a couple of pencils, too.

The short exchange, somewhat baffling to an outsider, offers some insights about Hanshaw Middle School and Vidal, its unconventional principal.

The "Fresno State" student knows the school's dress code prohibits attire from professional sports teams. Shirts bearing university logos, on the other hand, are encouraged, particularly those from the California State University campuses that Hanshaw's seven student "houses" are named after. Later in the day, the Fresno

State shirt will entitle the student to express-line service in the cafeteria and school store.

And while the sight of thirteen-year-olds voluntarily telling their principal they are being their personal best seems unusual, to put it mildly, it is not at all odd at Hanshaw. They are repeating a phrase that has become a school motto of sorts; the expression is heard during the morning announcements, in classrooms, on the school grounds, and in the gymnasium.

Interacting with students is what Vidal loves most about his job. If he is not handing out pencils, he is greeting students by name as they arrive at school, sitting in their classrooms offering encouragement, taking them to lunch to reward extra effort, or boarding every school bus on Friday afternoons to remind his students to be careful and, of course, to be their personal best, even at home. He is like the head cheerleader of a school that sees boosting its students' shaky self-esteem as a central function. "If I'm in my office," Vidal says, "I'm not doing my job."

Hanshaw Middle School opened in September 1991 in a depressed, gang-plagued neighborhood of South Modesto with a start-up enrollment of nearly eight hundred students. Almost everything that goes on inside the gleaming $13 million state-of-the-art facility shows Vidal's influence, from the interdisciplinary, project-based curriculum, to physical education classes that emphasize lifetime fitness skills over competition, to the school's lingo. (Students are called "citizens"; teachers, "community leaders.")

The campus, with its attractive two-story off-white buildings surrounding a grassy central courtyard, perfectly suits the principal's active style. On those rare occasions when he is in his office, Vidal can see everything going on in the central courtyard through large picture windows. Technological touches include telephones and computers in every classroom and a media center with videocassette recorders and CD-ROM players.

Hanshaw is the result of almost two years of planning by Vidal and his teachers, many of whom he hired months before the school actually opened. One of the first things Vidal did after being

selected to run the new school was to ask the state education department for a list of distinguished middle schools serving predominantly Hispanic populations. He visited some of these schools but
was not helped much by what he saw. The other programs were
either too much like traditional junior high schools or designed to
meet specific community needs.

The key to designing a successful school, Vidal concluded, is to
know one's community. So, he decided to convene town meetings
to discuss ideas for the new school. He also knocked on more than
five hundred doors, by his count, to find out more about the lives of
his prospective students—most of whom speak a language other
than English at home.

The South Modesto streets he canvassed are most definitely on
the wrong side of the tracks—or the Tuolumne River, in this case.
They are plagued with big-city problems like drugs, gangs, and
drive-by shootings. Predominantly Hispanic, South Modesto is
nothing like the all-American world portrayed in the movie *American Graffiti,* which was filmed in the city twenty years ago. Countless houses need repairs, or at least a paint job. And the residents
who own cars tend to drive models that the better-off residents
north of the river would have replaced long ago.

There are no paved sidewalks in this part of town; students walk
to school along dirt paths that turn to mud when it rains. The steep-
banked irrigation ditches that carry water to the area's immense
agricultural fields double as hazardous swimming holes on the many
days that the temperature tops a hundred degrees.

The residents of South Modesto fill the area's menial jobs; they
are the farm workers, day laborers, house cleaners, and the like.
Without any changes in the local schools, Vidal realized, the children in the neighborhood would likely languish in the same cycle
of poverty that has plagued their parents. He vowed not to turn out
another generation of second-class citizens.

"We have a lot of pent-up potential in these kids," the forty-year-
old principal says. All that is needed to unleash that potential, he
argues, is some encouragement, attention, and a predictable routine.

What Vidal hopes students will get from Hanshaw Middle School
is a sense of community missing from many of their lives. "That's
why we're the Hanshaw Titans," he notes. "A titan is an all-power-
ful person, one known for greatness of achievement. And I've told
my students that they all have sleeping titans inside of them, and
it's our job to wake them up."

· · · · · · · ·

South Modesto is a world (and three hundred miles) away from
affluent and conservative Orange County, California, where Charles
Vidal grew up. "It wasn't the real world," he says of his childhood
stomping grounds.

Vidal had planned to become a lawyer, but a part-time college
job as a junior high school coach changed his mind. He went into
teaching in the mid 1970s, landing a position as an English and history teacher at a low-income, inner-city high school in Riverside,
a city in southern California. It was that first teaching job, Vidal
recalls, that gave him "a real sense of the power of education and
how you can affect individuals and turn them around."

After five years in Riverside, Vidal moved to Modesto, a relatively poor city of 172,000 in the arid farming country east of San
Francisco, to become dean of students at Modesto High School. He
later became the school's assistant principal. Eventually, Vidal was
made principal of the district's alternative education center, which,
by the time he was tapped to head Hanshaw, was serving almost four
thousand K–12 students who could not make it in a regular classroom setting.

During his tenure at the alternative school, Vidal conducted a
research project that altered his outlook on schooling and later
influenced the design of the program at Hanshaw Middle School.
Troubled by a study showing that more than half of the Hispanic
students in the district never finish high school, he requested and
won a private grant to examine the problem. He hired a half-dozen

paraprofessionals to round up dropouts so he could talk to them about their experience in school. When he asked these youngsters why they left school, one answer came through loud and clear, Vidal says: "I don't see how what you're teaching me applies to my life; it has no meaning to me."

"It wasn't because teachers weren't working hard to develop lessons," Vidal says. What they were failing to do was show students why they should learn the material. "If you cannot tell a student why they need to know it," he says, "you're wasting their time."

Armed with this nugget of truth, Vidal and his teachers developed a set of themes and projects for Hanshaw that are solidly rooted in the students' lives. On this June day, for example, students in one class deliver short speeches on contemporary issues, ranging from abortion and teenage pregnancy to poverty and racism. Another class discusses discrimination in apartment rentals and scans local newspaper classified advertisements to find an apartment that fits the theoretical budget their teacher has given them. In a third classroom, students prepare a time capsule, writing short essays that offer advice to the citizens of Modesto in the year 2022.

"We've got to deal with some real problems in South Modesto, so one of the emphases is to teach what's really relevant now," Vidal says. "Let's teach them about themselves and their community, the things they'll encounter."

• • • • • • •

By all accounts, young adolescents are at the most difficult period of childhood, a time of raging hormones characterized by a new-found interest in the opposite sex and a growing demand for independence, both at home and in school. To help their students through this trying time and provide a transition from the protective, self-contained classrooms of elementary school to the more rigid, departmentalized schedule of high school, Vidal and his colleagues followed the middle school model when designing Hanshaw.

Unlike the four other traditional junior high schools in Modesto, Hanshaw is divided into seven "houses," which are essentially schools within a school. The sixty to one hundred students in each house take all their classes together from four or five teachers. Rather than naming the houses after animals, letters, or colors, Vidal came up with the idea of linking each house to one of the many California State University campuses within a half-day's drive of Modesto. He arranged for all the students to visit their namesake universities, where they were hosted by a team of minority students. The field trips involved no homework, only a little imagination: Vidal simply wanted the youngsters to picture themselves as college students some day.

Despite California's booming Hispanic population, Hispanics account for only 3 percent of California State's graduates. Vidal wants to push that number up. He hopes his young teenagers will see that students go on to college because they aspire to challenging, rewarding careers. But even Vidal, in all his enthusiasm, did not realize just how great the leap to college may be for some of his students. When the buses set off for the campus visits, the teachers found that many of the youngsters had never even been on a freeway, much less a university campus.

The teachers within each house at Hanshaw share a common daily planning period. During this first year, however, that time would have been more appropriately called a designing period, since Vidal basically set his teachers loose to create their curriculum from scratch. "Textbook learning is an insult," Vidal says. "Teachers are handed a textbook that they had nothing to do with developing; they're given a teacher's edition; they're given a sequence for learning; they're given the questions; they're given tests. We find security in teaching as we've been taught, but it's not meaningful to the kids, and in the long run, we're losing them."

Rather than leading students sequentially through huge amounts of material with the textbook as the guide, Vidal and his teachers decided to approach learning through a series of broad, interdisciplinary themes. "I told teachers that we weren't going to be in this just to cover material," Vidal explains. "We're not going to teach everything. Rather than doing twenty-seven things half-assed, we're going to do six or eight things really well."

Many of the themes were developed almost by accident, says seventh grade teacher Jeff Albritton. Teachers, he notes, spent countless hours at home devising ways to make the material relevant and stimulating. At one point during the year, Albritton turned his classroom into a medieval castle as part of a unit on the Renaissance.

Unlike most schools, Hanshaw encourages its teachers to do more than lecture. All of the classes center on projects; team teaching and cooperative learning are the norm. Vidal hates to see his teachers talking for more than fifteen minutes an hour, so the rooms are noisy places, buzzing with group activities. "We don't have one teacher and a room full of spectators," Vidal says. "That's a baseball game."

The seventh grade is structured around two eighty-eight-minute interdisciplinary core classes, one covering math and science, the other English and social studies. Vidal and his staff created a different schedule for the eighth graders, hoping to prepare them for the more departmentalized regimen of high school. These students attend forty-four-minute classes in each of the four core subjects, but their teachers, like the seventh grade teachers, still attempt to link subjects together.

This year, the seventh grade core teachers, in particular, devised some imaginative lessons. Mike Brennan, a first-year teacher and Modesto city councilor, came up with the idea of having his class prepare a meal to feed the entire school and surrounding community. As the project grew, it drove the class's curriculum for more than a month. Students contacted business leaders and others in the community, wrote letters to solicit donations, and worked in planning groups. The event was so successful that Brennan intends to repeat it this year. "It became a hands-on experience," he says. "Lots of people would say, 'That's not school.' But it's more real-life. It means more to them, and I think that will carry over a lot more."

The eighth grade teachers also managed to integrate subjects, although to a lesser extent. When the students in one house studied ecology in their science class, for example, they studied graphing and statistics in math; and during a unit on astronomy, the math classes turned to exponential numbers. Teachers also found ways to link science and social studies, discussing plate tectonics in one course and mapping in the other. There were obvious ways to connect social studies and literature; students read historical fiction related to the period they were studying.

Themes the teachers hope to raise in coming years include such broad topics as transitions, independence, justice, wellness, and social structures. The teachers are confident their jobs will be easier after the challenge of starting from scratch.

"This has been a hard year," seventh grade math and science teacher Edyth Curtis said in June. "After thirteen years of working with a curriculum, coming here was like being a first-year teacher all over again."

* * * * * * *

Hanshaw's innovative approach is not limited to the core academic classes. In physical education, for instance, the students are more likely to practice golf swings, swim in the Salvation Army pool across from the school, or work off their lunches with aerobic routines than compete in games of basketball or football. And the fitness-oriented approach seems to be paying off: teachers measured students' body-fat percentages at the beginning and end of the school year and found that almost three-quarters of the students had become more muscular. "At this age, self-improvement is important," P.E. teacher Toni Grgich says. "We're trying to get them to do stuff they can use forever and carry on into adult life."

Like the other teachers, Grgich finds small ways to link her course to what is going on in the other classes. When students study the Renaissance, for example, she teaches them jousting and juggling. Or she may have them recite the preamble to the Constitution while doing their daily jumping jacks. Unlike other schools where she has taught, Grgich notes, students at Hanshaw like to come to P.E.

Some of the school's most popular courses are those that are included in what is known around Hanshaw as the "exploratory wheel," a requirement for every student. The seventh grade exploratories cover arts and crafts, home economics, chorus, and industrial technology, while eighth graders delve into computers, industrial technology, study skills, and teen issues. "The whole idea behind middle school," Vidal says, "is to give students a taste of something, an experience of something that might get them to pursue it in high school."

That is definitely the idea behind Hanshaw's industrial-technology laboratory, developed by Robert Ransome, the state's 1990 Technology Teacher of the Year. His seventh grade classes are structured around five-day modules that expose students to a wide array of topics. On this particular day, his students are using computers to design floor plans for houses, making rubber stamps, building geodesic domes out of toothpicks, and designing their own business cards.

The eighth grade industrial-tech lab features longer, more advanced modules such as hydroponic gardening, working on a mock radio station, designing and building earthquake-proof towers, and bicycle repair. "Instead of just making bird cages, we're looking at the skills the students will need in the work force in the twenty-first century," says Ransome, who took a $9,000 pay cut to come to Hanshaw.

Students work in pairs as they progress through instruction manuals Ransome has prepared. To get a better sense of the working world, they keep time cards and can be temporarily "fired" (exiled to the back of the room for a day) if their attendance and work habits are not up to par. The care and attention they give their work is, in some respects, more impressive than the intricate projects they produce. Today, for example, Ransome's seventh graders are working intently, with little supervision, even though it is the last period of the day in the next to last week of the school year.

. . . .

No matter what the class, teachers and administrators at Hanshaw Middle School never miss an opportunity to offer students some positive reinforcement. Vidal, of course, is the number one booster, and the teachers never know what to expect from him. One day earlier this spring, during a visit to an eighth grade science classroom, Vidal asked the teacher to pick out two students who were doing good work. As a reward, he took the pair to the student store, opened it, gave them each a soft drink, and then walked them back to class, praising them all the way for their effort.

This constant boosterism—the pencils, the bus talks, the "be your personal best" slogan, and everything else—might seem "sappy" at a more affluent school, says Craig Johnson, the science teacher whose class Vidal visited that day. But not at Hanshaw. "A lot of these kids don't have an adult who spends two minutes with them all day long," Johnson says. "Their parents are working a tremendous amount, or they're from a single-parent family, or they're minus parents, or the parents have some overwhelming problem in their lives that leaves no time for kids. Just having an adult paying attention to them is unbelievable for some of these kids."

The students can tell that Vidal and the teachers care about them, says teacher Cheryl Green-Jenkins, and they appreciate it. Green-Jenkins' eighth grade English students start each class with a pledge to do their best, stay in school, graduate, and go on to college. Little things like that, she says, help students feel good about themselves, and those positive feelings make them believe they can do just about anything.

"The other thing we try to do here is point out the positive and not the negative in students," she adds. "It's so easy to tell somebody what they're doing wrong; you have to look a little harder to tell them what they're doing right. If you tell them what they're doing right, then they know what to do the next time."

It is a philosophy that students have picked up on. In a social studies class for students with limited English skills, two large groups of youngsters are reading aloud from a play about a citizen who tries to get a local law passed after he has a car accident. When one of the students stumbles over a line and a couple classmates laugh, others quickly reprimand them. "Don't laugh," they say. "It's not funny."

Even the teachers who express some skepticism about the heavy-handed attempts to boost students' self-esteem believe the school is making a difference for its young adolescents. "What really is going on at this school is simply a positive affirmation of these kids," says social studies teacher Robert Rosenthal. "You have to realize that academics is not necessarily their first priority. But always, whether or not they're performing what we want, we let them know they're worthwhile people. That's what they need to carry away from here. That's what self-esteem is really about at this site."

In similar, if more subtle, ways, Vidal lets the school's thirty-six teachers know that they are appreciated. He constantly offers encouragement and support, always urging them to "maintain the vision." He describes his faculty as "visionaries" who could not move beyond other principals' limited horizons. "You have some very creative teachers out there," he says, "but you have a lot of principals who are just managers and who are not taking the risks they need to take."

Vidal, by contrast, almost demands that his teachers take risks; he assured them early in the year that he would take responsibility for any failures and give them credit for every success. "If they don't fail at some things," he says, "then they know they're not taking enough risks, especially with this population. We want to sleep at night knowing we did everything we could do."

Vidal's trust in his teachers extends beyond the classroom; he gives them a major voice in school governance. Decision making at Hanshaw, for example, often consists of Vidal meeting with all the teachers in the "cafetorium," as the combined cafeteria-auditorium is known. "I go in there and we discuss problems," Vidal says. "I don't give them any solutions. I know where I want to go as an administrator, but my teams can give me a road map. I don't veto anything. And the reason is that they usually come up with better solutions than I do." In addition to their control over the curriculum, teachers have a say in everything from budgetary decisions to hiring new staff.

They clearly appreciate the principal's openness. Ransome, the industrial-technology teacher, calls Vidal "one of the most visionary and humane administrators I've ever worked for. This has been the nicest year I've ever had in twenty-five years of teaching."

Physical education teacher Grgich echoes those sentiments: "In all my years of teaching, this has been the most rewarding one. It's been a great year."

* * * * * * *

Still, not everyone in Modesto was as enthusiastic as Vidal and his teachers about the city's new middle school. In fact, the teachers say, some people in the community, both inside and outside the school system, resented spending so much money on "those" students in South Modesto.

"The other [junior high schools] really believed that once they got rid of our students, their scores would go up, and we would be over here in this big, fancy, expensive campus with scores that were in the toilet," Green-Jenkins says. "We knew within our school that we were being successful with the kids, but the measure of our success was going to be the numbers [on standardized tests]."

As it turned out, Hanshaw's seventh and eighth graders scored above grade level on the California Test of Basic Skills. In addition, average daily attendance at the school hovered around 98 percent, which Vidal calls an "unbelievable figure for a school like this." Likewise, the number of students failing at Hanshaw was the same as or lower than the number at the four junior high schools, and only three students were referred to alternative programs outside the school.

The teachers know that it is "the numbers" that attract the attention of the local news media, but they are also confident their students are doing well in ways no standardized test can measure. "The difference is the attitude of the kids toward the school and the feeling that they belong here," says Jerry Pasa, a seventh grade resource specialist at Hanshaw. "If that's the only difference we've made, then we've done a hell of a lot because that affects the social aspects of a person. And if you've got good social skills, you're going to make it through life."

Much of the initial resentment toward the school has dissolved as people have become more informed. But the teachers say that some critics remain convinced that the money spent on Hanshaw's students would have been better put to use in more advantaged neighborhoods.

Green-Jenkins believes that some teachers and administrators at other schools in the district perceive Hanshaw as a threat. "Hanshaw is trying some new things, and if those things are successful, people think they're going to be asked to implement them in their classrooms," she says. "There's that fear of change that we all experience."

She and the other teachers at Hanshaw would like to see other schools follow their lead. But for now, Hanshaw is the only school in town experimenting with a radically different approach to education. And that concerns the school's staff; they worry about how their students will fare when they get to high school.

Hanshaw's teachers plan to set up college clubs, based on the school's houses, at Downey High, where most of the middle school's eighth graders will go. The clubs, they hope, will help students stay in touch with each other and their former teachers. "We can still help them, even if they're not on campus," says teacher Mike Brennan.

On this spring day, as the first year of their experiment is winding down, Vidal and his teachers are already looking forward to their second year. The seventh graders will be back, and the curriculum will not seem quite so new.

"We're evolving," Vidal says. "We're proud of what we've accomplished, but we're more excited about what we're evolving into. Next year will be easier; this year we've really been writing the book."

Daniel Gursky

• • • • • • •

Charles Vidal and the other faculty members at Hanshaw Middle School have continued to improve the learning climate for their students. In February 1994, Hanshaw, with the help of a $500,000 Healthy Start grant, opened a school-based health clinic, which provides year-round medical, dental, and mental health services to Hanshaw students.

Danuta Offinowski

This chapter originally appeared as an article in *Teacher Magazine*, January 1993.

7

Blessed Are the Peacemakers

Robert DeSena

Robert DeSena remembers the time he and his then-fledgling organization were first put to the test. It was 1979. A fight that had broken out between African- and Italian-American youths at a luncheonette near John Dewey High School in the Bensonhurst section of Brooklyn, New York, escalated to include contingents of Asian and Hispanic students. It looked like the altercation was about to erupt into a much larger incident.

At a critical moment, English teacher DeSena and members of a club he had started four years earlier at Dewey, called the Council for Unity, brought the leaders of each faction together in the school cafeteria and offered them a choice: they could either face the disciplinary action of school administrators and the police, or they could join the council and work out the conflict there.

DeSena had founded the council in 1975 to promote positive relations among students from different racial and ethnic backgrounds and to provide an environment where students could resolve their conflicts peacefully. This incident was its first major challenge.

The leaders of the fighting factions opted to work with the council, and the confrontation was defused. DeSena's victory drew accolades and attracted attention to the small experiment under way at Dewey. Today, the council has become a fixture in twenty-seven schools in New York City: nineteen in Brooklyn, five in Queens, and three in Manhattan. By all accounts, Robert DeSena and his Council for Unity are making a difference.

"It used to be a club, and then it became an organization, and now it's become a movement," DeSena, a stocky, dark-haired man of Italian ancestry, says in his heavy Brooklyn accent. If you take kids who have a conflict to resolve and bring them together every day, he says, "something's going to happen. They just forget their ethnicity, and they begin to connect as human beings."

DeSena and the council have their work cut out for them. In recent years, Bensonhurst and other neighborhoods in Brooklyn have been the sites of nationally publicized incidents of racial violence.

In 1986, Michael Griffith, age twenty-three, and two other African Americans stopped at a pizzeria in Howard Beach, a mostly white neighborhood, after their car broke down nearby. They were confronted by a group of white men outside the pizzeria, and Griffith was chased onto the Belt Parkway where he was struck by a passing car and killed.

Then, in the summer of 1989, Yusef Hawkins, a sixteen-year-old African American from the East New York section of Brooklyn, came with three friends to the predominantly white Bensonhurst to buy a used car. They were confronted by an angry group of young white men, and one of them shot and killed Hawkins. In the weeks that followed, black political and religious leaders led protest marches through the streets of Bensonhurst, where they were derided with racial jeers from hostile crowds of whites filling the sidewalks.

In the summer of 1991, several nights of violence erupted in another Brooklyn neighborhood, Crown Heights, after Gavin Cato, a seven-year-old African-American boy, was struck and killed by a car driven by a Hasidic rabbi. During a heated clash between Hasidic Jews and African Americans, Yankel Rosenbaum, a twenty-nine-year-old Australian rabbinical student, was stabbed to death.

"We have kids shooting at each other because one group lives in private houses and the other lives in apartments," says Edward Muir, director of the United Federation of Teachers' school safety department. "Or one group lives on one side of the avenue, and another group lives on the other."

Race, he says, is yet another potential source of conflict. "Any difference," Muir warns, "can be a cause of war here."

In such an environment, he says, the work of a peer mediation group, like the Council for Unity, "is an important piece of the solution."

• • • • • • •

It is an early fall day, and the Council for Unity's office at Dewey High School, a three-story building located in the southern tip of Brooklyn, is abuzz with activity. Several students are diligently pecking away at electric typewriters. Another answers a constantly ringing telephone: "Hello, Council for Unity, how can I help you?" Others are scattered, chatting casually in small groups—groups notable for their racial mix. Dewey's population is 34 percent African American, 30 percent white, 23 percent Hispanic, and 13 percent Asian.

In between conversations, Robert DeSena spots several unfamiliar students and walks over to shake their hands. "You must be new. Hi, I'm Bob DeSena," he says warmly. He calls out to another student, "Hey, why don't you show these kids some of the council yearbooks and get them oriented?"

It is this kind of welcome and friendly atmosphere that draws students to the Council for Unity. They are made to feel as if they belong. "I heard about it when I came here for orientation," says Indigo Bethea, a fourteen-year-old sophomore at Dewey. "It seemed like the friendliest place in the whole high school." Tiffany Crespi, also a sophomore, recalls walking by the council office at Dewey and thinking "everyone seemed to be like one big family."

"If you look at what's going on in this society, families are under siege," DeSena says. "Schools have been asked to compensate for that, but, for the most part, they can't because schools are too big and too impersonal." That is where the Council for Unity comes in.

"We're in competition with gangs and posses, which require a lot of conformity from kids," DeSena explains. "They have to become, speak, dress, act a certain way." But in the council, he says, "students can be themselves. That's extremely difficult, if not impossible, in the streets, where you have to be a clone of the clique you're in. You know, you join a gang, you get a jacket, you get your colors, whatever."

In response, the council offers an alternative collection of customs and has created its own symbols, jackets, and colors. It also offers students a place to hang out at school that is unlike most institutional classrooms. The walls of the council's headquarters at Dewey, for example, are painted with student murals that depict key events in council history, such as the 1979 dispute, and inspirational leaders, such as Martin Luther King, Jr.

Everything here in Room 102, in fact, seems to be painted with symbolic imagery; even a storage cabinet is covered with a sea of multicolored handprints. The council, asserts DeSena, is "a culture. It's got its heroes; it's got its traditions; it's got founders; it's got a value system; it's got a philosophy."

"It's kind of like a good gang," explains Justine Luongo, the council's director of program activities and a 1985 alumna of Dewey. "The sense of commitment that it instills in students, and the feeling that once you are a member you are a member for life, gives them a sense of self-worth."

Luongo, who was a member of the council as a student, says the program turned her life around. "My first year at John Dewey High School was a complete disaster," she says. She came to Dewey from a very strict parochial school and, unable to cope with the high school's less structured environment, began to cut classes and get in trouble.

"A friend of my mother's, who also serves as a custodian at the school, grabbed me by the scruff of my neck and took me to Room 102," she recalls. "I saw a teacher working side by side with students on a project, and, from where I was standing, that's not something

I wanted to do." At that point in her life, Luongo says, she "just wanted to hang out, and that would have been fine." But something clicked, she remembers. "I said, 'Hey, I'm going to give it a try.'"

Through her experiences as a member of the council, Luongo learned that teachers did not always have to be in a position of authority to get her respect. "They could be your friend, and they could be your teacher, too," she says. "And they don't always have to be in front of a chalkboard."

At most participating schools, the Council for Unity operates primarily as an extracurricular activity; chapters meet during students' free periods or after school. But, at several sites, it has also become part of the fabric of the academic curriculum. At Dewey, for example, students on the council can receive social studies credit for their participation. These students spend one day each week outside of the building working on a community service project (the flexible schedule at Dewey makes this possible) and keep a weekly journal describing their activities. They are also required to work for one of the council's committees and submit a written evaluation of their experience at the end of the quarter.

A primary philosophical tenet of the council is that the chapters be student directed. Teachers are involved but in a supportive, rather than an authoritarian, capacity. "The students make a lot of mistakes," DeSena says. "They're supposed to. That's how they learn; that's how they get confidence. The council is kind of applied citizenship. Kids are taking the concepts of government and the theories of democracy and cooperation and applying them."

The actual student leadership structure varies greatly from chapter to chapter. At Dewey, the council is overseen by a six-member executive board and eight committees. The governing framework of the chapter at Susan B. Anthony Intermediate School in Queens, however, is more informal: there are no officers, and most decisions are reached by consensus.

One of the council's major priorities is to teach students peer mediation skills. "It's one of the sexiest things right now," DeSena notes wryly. But peer mediation training alone, he says, is not enough because, at the end of each school day, students return home to the same old environment and value system. "Resolving conflict is the first step," DeSena says, "but it can't be the first and the last step."

In an effort to melt the prejudices at the heart of many conflicts, council chapters host an array of multicultural events. Last year, the council chapter at Susan B. Anthony, for example, held a Passover Seder, took part in the African-American cultural festival Kwanzaa, hosted a "Brotherhood and Sisterhood Dance," and learned about Irish traditions on St. Patrick's Day.

The hope is that exposing students to the traditions of other cultures will foster greater understanding and tolerance. The St. Patrick's Day gathering, notes chapter adviser and assistant principal Anne Johnson, eventually evolved into a discussion about New York City Mayor David Dinkins' decision not to march in the St. Patrick's Day parade because of the exclusion of gay and lesbian groups.

With a student body that is 54 percent African American, 25 percent Hispanic, 18 percent Asian, and 3 percent white (representing some fifty-three different countries), the Anthony school "is a real United Nations," Johnson says. And often, she adds, "it's very hard to get people to coalesce around common goals when they are coming from so many different directions."

Last June, the school's council members performed a play called *A Flower for Dorothy*, a twist on *The Wizard of Oz*, in which the central character, a young girl, lives in a neighborhood that is changing racially. When Dorothy's parents discover she has become friends with children from different ethnic and racial groups, they become upset and send her to bed. Then, in a dream, she goes on a quest to bring four knights in a racially divided forest together.

"It's like a journey she takes to find out about different races," explains eighth grader Lisa Henderson. "And, in the end, she learns that it doesn't matter what they look like; people are the same."

The play, which DeSena penned in 1983, is one of twenty-six he has written for council chapters to perform. Drama has become a central part of the council's program, DeSena says, because "every piece of multicultural curriculum I've ever seen is boring; it's used to beat kids over the head to appreciate other cultures. And, in a lot of cases, it's resented." Drama, he says, not only makes the topic more fun, but it also teaches students a variety of practical skills. He quickly rattles off a list: "They learn to articulate; they learn blocking; they learn how to project; they also learn about writing and choreography."

Community service is an equally important component of the council's agenda. This past fall, a chapter in the Fort Hamilton section of Brooklyn held food and toy drives for the needy. Students at Dewey have operated a senior citizen escort service and taken patients at the South Brooklyn Psychiatric Center out for lunch and bowling. They have also run a recycling program and collected clothes and food for victims of Hurricane Andrew.

"The whole notion of being responsible for and to the society you live in is key," DeSena says. "We just went through two decades of self-absorption and self-centeredness. How are we going to get young people involved in the political process if we divorce schools from life, especially from community life?"

This school year, DeSena and the other teachers who advise the various council chapters are working with restaurants throughout the city to set up a "dining network." Each participating restaurant will host a free dinner for about fifteen families of council members. Breaking bread with neighbors from different backgrounds in an intimate setting, DeSena asserts, is one way to begin dismantling the racial and cultural barriers in each community. "Nothing gets done unless it's personalized," he says. "You're more apt to work for change with people you know and like than for an idea."

* * * * * * *

Born and raised in Brooklyn's Bay Ridge section, DeSena attended Roman Catholic primary and secondary schools. After graduating from St. John's University in 1963, he earned a master's degree in English at New York University. He taught at Eastern District High School and East New York High School of Transit Technology before moving to Dewey in 1970. During his tenure at the school, he has seen seven principals come and go.

DeSena's understanding of the psychology of urban adolescent culture is rooted in experience; he was deeply involved in gang life as a teenager. "I'm an ex–street guy," he acknowledges. "I can't afford to pass judgment on anybody because I used to be just like them." He went through the typical rites of puberty and manhood in a gang, he says—"fighting and drinking and playing around with women and all that."

Most of his peers did not aspire to finish school or get a job. "If you're at school after sixteen, at least back in my days, it was like, 'What the hell is wrong with you?'" he says. "If you work for a living, you're lame."

Eventually, DeSena began to see the darker side of gang life. "The laws that govern your life, which you never really acknowledge or are aware of, kick in and destroy you," he says. Back then, heroin was the drug of choice, and watching it destroy some of his friends' lives, DeSena says, ultimately saved his own. "It just decimated street gangs all over the city," he recalls. "It was like living in the movie *Invasion of the Body Snatchers*. You thought you knew somebody, and then, all of a sudden, there was something else living inside of them, that alter ego that heroin created."

As a student at St. John's, DeSena turned to religion in the hopes of straightening out his life. "Like everything I do, I did this to extreme," he chuckles. "And that wasn't too productive for me either. I think you end up trying to be perfect when you get religious and you want other people to be, too."

Also at this time, a man about ten years DeSena's senior befriended him and helped keep him on the right track. This friend had married young and did not go to college; as a result, he continually encouraged DeSena to stick with his studies. "He was really trying to make sure that I didn't follow in his footsteps, and he made me look at my friends in a much different light," DeSena says. "He kind of showed me that they weren't free, that they'd never be free, that the gang rules."

What DeSena did not know, however, was that his friend was struggling with a heroin addiction. The friend called him one night, upset and wanting to meet. "I didn't show up," DeSena says. "And that night, he killed himself, jumped in front of a train." The next day was April Fools' Day. "When they told me he died, I thought it was a joke," DeSena remembers. "It wasn't."

It was then that DeSena decided to become a teacher, hoping that he might be able to prevent others from suffering a similar fate. "I never forgot the street," he says, "and I never forgot my commitment to kids who were never called on in class, who didn't quite fit the so-called norm, who didn't look socially or politically correct, who were outlaws and outsiders. Those were the kids that I wanted to go back and redeem because I felt I owed it to my friends who weren't around anymore."

As he began his teaching career, DeSena deliberately sought out the "difficult" students, and he discovered he enjoyed working with them the most. "The tougher the kids, the worse the kids, the better I liked it," he says.

For many years, DeSena's signature English class at Dewey was a course in mythology. He sees many parallels between the class— which featured an eclectic mix of Native American, African, Eastern Mediterranean, and Greek myths—and his work at the council. "The kids," he says, "were able to look at the common themes that govern life and govern all mythology, which forced them to look inward and look at themselves and ask, 'Am I happy?' 'Where am I going?' 'What's the purpose of life?' 'How will these myths help me get a richer vision of what life is all about?' I think the council answers some of those mythological questions. We know why we are here. We know what our mission is. And we have discovered our happiness pursuing it."

Each year, as DeSena's responsibilities at the council have grown, his teaching load has correspondingly decreased. This year, for the first time in twenty-seven years, he is not teaching any English classes, a decision he calls one of the most painful of his life. Still, he does not feel that he has truly left teaching. "I'm teaching now. It's just that I'm teaching citizenship; I'm teaching politics; I'm teaching organizational health," he says. "The Council for Unity is a culture, and I am a resource teacher for that culture."

◆　◆　◆　◆　◆　◆　◆

Clad in a purple, black, and jade running suit and a spotless pair of white New Balance sneakers, DeSena heads out of the council headquarters with a visitor for a quick lunch break. As he passes through the school's hallways, he stops to chat with a group of students collecting signatures for a petition that criticizes a board of education proposal to make AIDS education classes focus primarily on abstinence. He signs the petition and promises to tell council members about it upon his return.

Seated in an Italian restaurant not far from the school, DeSena says the rapid growth of the council is taking its toll on him and the staff. "It used to be so simple," he sighs. "We have a lot of stress on us, a lot of stress."

The major push to expand began in 1986, after the death of Michael Griffith in Howard Beach. Griffith's death was not the first racially provoked killing in Brooklyn in recent years; in 1982, an African-American transit worker named Willie Turks had been beaten to death in Bensonhurst by a gang of young white men. After that tragedy, the neighborhood came together to condemn the individuals who committed the crime. But the Howard Beach incident was different, DeSena says.

It was one of the first major incidents to receive a lot of national publicity. Previously, the community had the illusion, DeSena says, "that this incident with Willie Turks was an aberration. You think there's a bunch of isolated punks; they beat up a black guy. And you think, 'That's really not this city.' But, when it happens again three or four years later, and again two years later, you can't really say this is an isolated incident."

Following Griffith's death, the National Ethnic Coalition of Organizations (NECO), an umbrella group of some sixty-three prominent ethnic associations, began searching for successful community programs that were trying to address race relations. The United Federation of Teachers (UFT), New York City's teachers' union, a longtime supporter of the Council for Unity, recommended it to coalition officials. "The council is a very good example of what can be done," UFT President Sandra Feldman says. "It gives you such a feeling of hope and restores your belief in the fact that we can teach racial tolerance and understanding. It does it in a way that also helps students develop strong relationships with each other, which they carry with them into adulthood."

But DeSena and his students were not sure the council could be replicated elsewhere. "It was a crisis for us," DeSena confesses. In the end, NECO gave the council $25,000 to start a chapter at Mark Twain Junior High School. If it worked there, then they would take it to other schools in Brooklyn's Community District 21. "It just snowballed," DeSena says.

Today, there is a council chapter in almost every school in District 21. And DeSena and other council supporters see the district as a model for further expansion because children can participate in the program from elementary school through high school. "We have to reach the children at such a young age," says Domenic Recchia, vice president of the District 21 board of education and a Dewey and Council for Unity alumnus. "If we can catch them at the beginning and teach them to respect one another, they can learn to get along better later in life."

Since receiving the initial $25,000 grant, the council has forged a strong partnership with NECO and one of its member organizations, the Coalition of Italo-American Associations. The two groups have played a pivotal role in drumming up support for the project on the New York City board of education and among the business community and labor unions. Together, they are trying to raise $1 million to build an "intergroup relations" center at Dewey. The center would serve as the new headquarters for the Council for Unity and house a multicultural library, classroom space, conference rooms, and a computer center. DeSena hopes it will become a "living laboratory" of the council's work and a resource center for the community.

The council is continuing to grow on other fronts, as well. Its alumni association, incorporated in 1983, today has about seven hundred members. And last year, a new chapter for parents of council members was established.

In the near future, DeSena hopes to see the program expand into the city's two other boroughs—the Bronx and Staten Island—as well as into parts of southern New York state and Long Island and, eventually, across the entire country. But, at the present time, the council has neither the staff nor the resources to meet the increasing demand and will need to solicit outside funds before it can continue to grow. "The problem we're having is that the program has been so successful that we can't accommodate the number of kids who want to get in," DeSena says. "And I still don't know what the answer is."

Currently, new chapters must come up with an initiation fee of $25,000, which covers the program's administrative costs, training for the chapter's advisers, curriculum materials, other council resources, and supplies for special events. Although the fee drops to $18,000 in the second year and $7,500 the third, schools are finding it an arduous task to procure these funds during a period of widespread state and city budget cutbacks. Yung Wing Elementary School in Chinatown, for example, was only able to afford the program through a grant from the Fund for New York City Public Education.

The council staff is grappling with challenges on other fronts, as well. Some are rooted in external factors, which it has little power to change. For example, the enduring patterns of de facto segregation in the city translate into extremely homogeneous student bodies in some neighborhoods, which, in turn, make it difficult for chapters in schools in those areas to conduct an authentic multicultural program.

At Yung Wing Elementary, 90 percent of the student body is Asian. So, to compensate for its lack of racial and ethnic diversity, the council there started a pen-pal program with Public School 177 in Brooklyn, a more racially mixed school. The program is supplemented with occasional student visits. DeSena acknowledges, however, that this will have a limited impact, especially compared with schools where children have day-to-day contact with peers from a broad range of racial and ethnic groups.

• • • • • • •

It is easy to find fans of Robert DeSena in almost every corner of New York City's school system. No one seems to have anything but kind words to say about him, a remarkable feat in a sprawling urban school district known for its frequent and heated political skirmishes.

"Bob's a dynamic individual, and he's very streetwise; he knows just how the kids feel," says Richard Grace, honorary chairman of the ethnic coalition. "Because he can communicate with them, I think that's part of his greatest asset to the program."

Many say it is DeSena's dogged determination that has made the council a success. "He doesn't know how to say no," says Johnson, assistant principal at Susan B. Anthony. "If there's something you need, he'll find it for you." When her students were unable to attend a council event in Brooklyn, Johnson recalls, DeSena managed to conjure up several buses to transport them there.

Others cite his infectious élan and his undying energy. "Bob has this sincere passion for the organization that has caused it to grow tremendously," says Luongo, the council's program director. "This is his life. Everything about Bob is Council for Unity since the time he started it."

DeSena is also lauded for his sensitivity and concern. Johnson tells how DeSena, whom she has only known on a professional level for about a year, recently came to the funeral of her sister, who died of cancer and left behind a young daughter for Johnson to raise. "When I saw him walk into the funeral parlor, I was so surprised," she says. "Bob said to me, 'When something happens to one of us, it happens to all of us.' That touched me so personally."

In 1992, DeSena received more formal recognition. He was one of four individuals honored at an annual awards ceremony held by the Boston-based Petra Foundation. This relatively new foundation was created as a memorial to Petra Shattuck, a teacher, lawyer, and human rights activist, who died of a cerebral hemorrhage in 1988 at forty-six. Each year, the foundation presents several $5,000 awards to individuals whose work either promotes racial justice; protects the autonomy of individuals, groups, or communities; or defends freedom of speech and expression.

"It was very clear that [the council] had done something remarkable and that he'd started an organization that was larger than himself," says Mark Munger, a management consultant who serves on the foundation's board. "By force of personality, by force of character, he has taught his students that there are different ways to solve problems other than blowing someone's head off."

But perhaps the best measure of the Council for Unity's success is the fact that Dewey, the organization's home base, has experienced no major acts of racial violence since its inception in 1975. Even in the wake of the Howard Beach and Bensonhurst incidents and, more recently, during the Los Angeles riots, the school has remained a relative island of calm.

"I'm the luckiest guy in the world," DeSena muses. "I find it ironic that I'm getting paid to do this kind of work because if I was a rich man, I'd do it for nothing. If my kids were told they would have to go back and just live with their own kind, I think it would kill them. They have really learned something that is overpowering."

. . . .

DeSena tells a story that seems to capture both the hope and the frustration of the Council for Unity's work.

Outside the administrative offices at Dewey High School is a 140-foot planter. Back in 1982, members of the council, noticing that the planter was overrun with weeds, decided to turn it into a garden, to leave behind a living symbol of racial harmony for future generations of students to cultivate and fertilize. They planted evergreens—junipers, rhododendrons, and azaleas—and representatives of each ethnic and racial group in the council planted a weeping cherry tree. The students viewed them not just as plants, DeSena says, but also as symbols.

"The kids wanted to get weeping trees because they wanted to show the state of the world when nations are divided," he explains. "They were going to plant them really close so their branches intermingled. But they decided to plant them farther apart, to show the kids who followed them that you can't get brotherhood and sisterhood without labor."

They called it the "Garden of Nations."

Seven years later, the murder of Yusef Hawkins by a gang of predominantly Italian-American youths ripped Bensonhurst apart. DeSena says the killing devastated the council members.

When school opened that fall, the students returned to Dewey to find that the two weeping cherry trees planted by the council's African- and Italian-American students had withered and died. "We came back a couple of days after the tragedy and were just dumbfounded," DeSena recalls. "Of course, it's coincidental; we're not into parapsychology here. But just the coincidence of it wasn't lost on anyone, believe me."

DeSena's students immediately held a fundraiser to buy two new weeping cherry trees, so the African- and Italian-American members of the council could together plant new trees to replace the old ones.

The evergreens, DeSena is quick to note, are also still thriving in the Garden of Nations today. The students selected the evergreens, he says, "because they wanted to show a sense of permanence, that the longing for harmony and for peace is constant."

"We may not get there," he adds, "but we'll sure keep trying."

Meg Sommerfeld

• • • • • • •

The Council for Unity has now expanded into all of New York City's five boroughs, with chapters in thirty-five schools. The program also has taken root in a number of schools outside New York. Robert DeSena continues to serve as the council's executive director.

♦ ♦ ♦ ♦ ♦ ♦ ♦

Danuta Offinowski

This chapter originally appeared as an article in *Teacher Magazine*, March 1993.

8

Overnight Sensation

Kay Toliver

U ntil recently, Kay Toliver was one of the best-kept secrets of
Manhattan's East Harlem Tech Middle School. The veteran
math teacher was highly regarded within her school for her innovative teaching methods and leadership qualities, but, like most
teachers, Toliver had spent her career in relative obscurity. Not that
she craved recognition. For Toliver, teaching is a reward in and of
itself. "I love doing it," she says. "I've never wanted to become an
administrator. I want to be a teacher."

But one of her colleagues, special education teacher Elba Marrero, wanted the world to know about Kay Toliver. Marrero saw a
notice about the Disney American Teacher Awards in a newspaper,
and she thought, "I want to get Kay to do it. She just has no sense of
how great she is."

There was a small problem, however: Toliver was reluctant to
enter the competition. "I'm not really into contests," she told her
friend. But Marrero would not take no for an answer. "I kept hounding her and hounding her until she applied," Marrero says. Putting
it off until the last minute, Toliver had to run to the post office so
that her application would meet the March 9, 1992, deadline.

About a month and a half later, Toliver got the good news: she
had been chosen one of three finalists in the competition's mathematics division. Toliver and the thirty-five other finalists from all
across the country were to fly, at Disney's expense, to Los Angeles

for the awards ceremony, to be broadcast live on the Disney Channel on December 6. When the evening finally arrived, millions were watching as Toliver, elegantly dressed in a gold-and-black sequined gown, was named the outstanding math teacher for 1992. (Rafe Esquith, a Los Angeles elementary school teacher, was selected as the overall winner.) As she stood at the podium clutching her award, Toliver told the audience, "I know that back in New York, I have all my students at East Harlem Tech/P.S. 72 watching." Then she looked directly at the camera and said, "Alright! I won!" Shifting her gaze, she added, "But do you know who I won for? I've won for my students—the ones who come to math class and don't like math. And the ones who leave loving math."

Toliver returned to New York on cloud nine—and with $2,500 in prize money for herself and $2,500 for her school. "It was like a dream," she says of her experience in Los Angeles. "Teachers don't expect to be greeted at the airport with a limousine." When Toliver returned to East Harlem Tech, the students and teachers treated her like a star. And the city council of New York went so far as to declare December 16 "Kay Toliver Day." To some of Toliver's students, the teaching profession has suddenly taken on a new luster. "I've never had kids who wanted to become teachers," Toliver notes with surprise.

The Disney award meant a lot to Toliver, but it was not the only honor she received in 1992. In September, she was named one of 216 Presidential Award winners by the National Science Foundation. The award, which comes with a $7,500 school grant, recognizes outstanding teachers of science and mathematics and encourages them to serve as role models for their colleagues and to advance education reforms in their disciplines. "I'm quite proud to be representing this district," Toliver says. "I'm proud because I'm a minority and a woman."

Also that year, the Foundation for Advancements in Science and Education, which had previously collaborated with renowned teacher Jaime Escalante to create the PBS math series *Futures*, selected Toliver to participate in a forthcoming multimedia math project. It will use computer and video technology to bring Toliver's teaching methods to other teachers.

Toliver, forty-seven, is somewhat amazed by all the attention she has been getting lately. After twenty-six years of teaching, she's suddenly being treated like an overnight sensation. "People," she says, "want to know, 'Where did she come from?' Well, I've been here all the time!"

* * * * * * *

East Harlem has long been one of New York City's poorest neighborhoods. It offers a stark contrast to the affluence of the Upper East Side, which lies directly to the south. About 120,000 people live in East Harlem; two-thirds are Hispanic, and the rest are mostly African-American.

East Harlem Tech is actually a school within a school, in this case P.S. 72, a red-brick structure built in 1924 to accommodate the tide of European immigrants then pouring into the area. Originally designed as an annex to a much larger building across the street, it is now something like an afterthought, the older school having been closed years ago. In fact, the American flag flying above the school's entrance on 104th Street is about the only indication that P.S. 72 is anything other than an old factory or warehouse. The neighborhood is like much of East Harlem: a combination of decaying brownstones, shops, and public housing projects.

In 1970, when New York City's massive school system was carved into thirty-two separate community school districts, P.S. 72, an elementary school, became part of Community School District 4. Four years later, the district's schools ranked at the very bottom in reading and mathematics. Less than 16 percent of its students were reading at or above grade level. With nothing to lose and everything to gain, District 4's leaders decided to create a number of theme-based alternative schools and then allow parents to choose which ones they wanted their children to attend. Teachers were encouraged to design their own programs; Deborah Meier, a former kindergarten teacher, took over two floors of P.S. 171, a rundown elementary school, and opened Central Park East Elementary School. (Meier went on to become one of New York's most famous educators, and Central Park East now comprises three schools, from kindergarten through twelfth grade. In January 1993, the New York City Board of Education approved a plan that will bring choice to all of the city's elementary and intermediate schools.)

By 1988, the proportion of District 4's students reading at or above grade level had climbed to 64.8 percent—a considerable improvement compared with 1974's figure but still below average for New York City. District officials are quick to point out other indicators that have gone up since the mid 1970s. According to Sy Fliegel, formerly the district's director of alternative education, in 1973 only ten students from District 4 were accepted into New York's specialized high schools (all of which require an entrance examination), while in 1988 more than 250 were admitted.

Although District 4 has been widely praised, particularly by advocates of school choice, for its innovations, skeptics have accused the district's boosters of distorting the truth. "While exaggerating the meager successes of District 4," writes former District 4 teacher Billy Tashman in *The New Republic*, "they have ignored some central facts: that the district's schools choose the kids as much as the other way around; that reading scores may have gone up, fueled by kids recruited from outside the district, but there is no evidence that general academic ability has improved; and that though students are attending more regularly, this is due less to choice than to the creation of small schools with a lot of autonomy—places that have improved students' lives a little bit."

East Harlem Tech is one of those "small schools with a lot of autonomy." Created in 1979 and located on P.S. 72's fifth floor, the school comprises seven teachers and 104 students, 85 percent of whom are Hispanic and 15 percent of whom are African-American. Math and science are clearly the focus, but students, who keep the same teachers for both seventh and eighth grades, must also take classes in social studies, communication arts, and computers. In addition, the school has a special education component. Students do choose to attend East Harlem Tech, but it is not as selective as some of District 4's other middle schools. Many of the students, in fact, grew up in the neighborhood and attended P.S. 72. "We take a wide range," says Principal Susan Siegel, who also directs P.S. 72. "We sort of give ourselves a 'curve' of students. I'd like to take all the best, but I can't do that. I take the ones who want to be here, and if they're not that good, we'll work with them, and they'll get better."

Perhaps because of its small size, East Harlem Tech has been spared much of the violence that has affected so many of the nation's inner-city schools. "This is a safe haven for junior high kids," Toliver says. "You don't have to worry about weapons here. You don't have to worry about viciousness here. They're sweet kids. People say, 'Oh, you teach in East Harlem! Aren't you scared to go to school?' No, I'm happy to come to school. We walk in the community. The people know me. I used to live around here. So it doesn't bother me. Of course, I know there's a lot of danger out there, but not in this building."

Toliver, who now lives in the Bronx, near Yankee Stadium, arrives at East Harlem Tech every morning about 8:00. She could take the subway to get there, but she admits, somewhat reluctantly, that she chooses not to. "I take a cab," she says, "because I'm always carrying big bags. I'm always bringing in something, and these bags are heavy. It wouldn't take me that much longer on the subway, but when you're constantly carrying packages, it's very bad, and it's crowded. So I do take a cab to work. I figure I can give myself that luxury because I don't have any big vices!" She laughs. "Sometimes the kids think I'm rich because I ride in a taxi cab, but I tell them no, I'm really quite poor. This is my one luxury."

• • • • • • •

To reach Toliver's classroom, Room 504, one has to walk up a narrow, dark stairwell; the school has no elevator. In the hallway outside her room is a bulletin board that says, "Congratulations Ms. Toliver," followed by a list of her recent honors. The walls of Room 504 are painted two shades of yellow, which helps brighten the place up. Three rows of fluorescent lights hang from the high ceiling. Although the temperature outside is only in the fifties, the radiators are blasting out heat, so all the windows have been opened to bring some cool air into the classroom. But that merely creates another problem for Toliver and her students: the constant sound of traffic on Lexington Avenue and commuter trains on the nearby elevated tracks.

It is 9:30 A.M. and time for Toliver's weekly eighth grade math lab. As the students drift into the room and take their seats, Toliver, wearing a white lab coat with "Holt, Rinehart and Winston" on the pocket, writes on the blackboard, "Do now. Describe a bridge!" Then, in a vertical column, she writes,

Problem:

Hypotheses:

Materials:

Procedure:

Observation:

Conclusion:

Turning to her students, who are seated at desks that have been bunched together to form small groups, Toliver reminds them of the "alien" who had visited the class the week before. It seems the alien had no idea what "area" and "perimeter" meant, and it was the students' task to explain the terms. "Well, now that same alien is here," Toliver says, "and that alien does not know what a bridge is. Would you very quickly write a description of a bridge for someone who has never seen one before?"

As they write, Toliver moves around the classroom, prodding her students in a friendly manner. After about ten minutes, she says, "OK. Pencils down. Now, who can tell me what a bridge is?"

"A bridge is a flat surface that separates two places," one student offers. Says another, "A bridge connects two bodies of land."

"OK," Toliver says, "we've got a flat surface, and things go over it. What else would you tell a person who had never seen a bridge before?"

"Man-made or natural," answers one student.

"Would that help me in seeing it?" Toliver asks. "What else?"

"If it had water under it," another student replies.

Toliver, realizing her students are getting offtrack, attempts to redirect the conversation. "Someone mentioned shapes," she says. "Dominique, I think it was you. What did you say about the shapes used in bridges?" Several students shout out answers: "Triangles." "Rectangles."

The teacher asks the class if they have walked over any bridges recently. About half the students raise their hands. "Elizabeth, where was the bridge you walked over?"

Elizabeth: "The George Washington Bridge."

Toliver: "You walked over the George Washington Bridge? I would have been scared to death! Could you tell us what the George Washington Bridge looks like?"

Elizabeth: "Like any other bridge!"

Toliver: "Well, does it look like my bridge?"

The teacher holds up a bridge she has built, a two-foot-long model made of wooden triangles.

Most of the class members agree that Toliver's bridge does not look anything like the George Washington Bridge.

At this point, Toliver takes a slight detour, turning her math lab into a geography lesson. She asks if any of her students know which two bodies of land the George Washington Bridge connects. "Two boroughs," says one. "Manhattan and the Bronx," says another. Since no one seems to know, Toliver offers bonus points to any students who can come up with the correct answer.

"Anybody else been across a bridge lately, either by walking or by driving?" Toliver asks.

"The Verrazano Narrows Bridge," replies one student, but he does not know what it connects, and neither do any of his classmates. So a slightly exasperated Toliver gives it to them as another bonus question, telling them, "These are bridges you've been over, now come on!" Tomorrow, she says, they will walk over to the East River to look at the Wards Island Bridge. "And we'll see what other bridges we can see."

Finally, Toliver changes gears again. "OK, we keep coming back to this shape, the triangle," she says. "And that's your lab problem for today. Your problem is to discover why engineers, in designing bridges, tend to use triangular-shaped figures." She asks her students to first write down their hypotheses. "What's a hypothesis?" she asks. "A guess," a girl says. "What kind of guess?" Toliver asks. "An educated guess," the girl replies, correcting herself.

As she passes out the materials for the lab project—cardboard, scissors, paper fasteners—Toliver explains the lesson, using clear, direct language. "Cut the cardboard into one-inch strips. Work together at your tables. You will make triangular figures in which you will use the paper fasteners to connect the vertices. Then, you will make a quadrilateral in which you will connect the vertices with the paper fasteners, so that you will then have two figures. Once you've constructed these two figures, I want you to compare them and see if you can come up with the reason to explain why engineers use triangular figures in constructing bridges."

Toliver gives them thirty minutes to complete the task. The students get busy cutting the cardboard into strips, but it is tough because their scissors are inadequate and there are not enough to go around. ("I think all of our scissors are either begged, borrowed, or stolen," Toliver tells a visitor.) But they get the job done, and, slowly, the shapes begin to take form. As they work, Toliver—who seems physically incapable of standing in one place for more than a few seconds—darts around the classroom, making sure her students are completing the task. The noise level in the classroom jumps up a few notches. At one point, Toliver uses an old trick: She turns the lights on and off to get the students' attention. It works; they quiet down.

The students begin to ponder their creations. The triangles maintain their shapes, while the quadrilaterals are obviously too flimsy to use in building a bridge. Yet some students cannot quite articulate the difference.

Toliver asks the class to repeat her original question. "Now, who can give us the answer to that question, based on what we just did?"

One student says, "The triangle is sturdier than a quadrilateral." Another says, "A triangle gives more support." Still another points out that, if you want to use a rectangle to build something, you should add a cross support to turn it into two triangles.

Finally, Toliver says, "In math, therefore, we say that a triangle is a 'rigid' figure. Would you describe a quadrilateral as a 'rigid' figure?" In unison, the students reply, "No!"

Toliver has spent an entire class period letting her students discover a simple but important math concept. "They're used to somebody saying, 'A triangle is a rigid figure. It'll hold things up,' without really letting them see for themselves," she explains later. "Well, I want them to see for themselves."

. . . .

After the math lab, Toliver takes a few minutes to talk about her teaching style, a sort of "whole math" approach that she has developed through years of teaching in East Harlem. "I want to teach the whole child," she says. "I want them to start thinking and using some logical explanations for why things are the way they are and not just sitting back and waiting for the teacher to always communicate the idea. I like to use writing a lot because many of my kids are Spanish dominant, and they come in with poor writing skills. So this is another way to get them to express themselves, other than in the English classes. They have to realize that writing and explanation are part of the mathematical process. And that's why I wanted them to describe the bridge.

"I want them to find out that math can be a pleasurable experience. That's the whole idea. Math class shouldn't be something that they fear coming to. My greatest joy is just seeing my students enjoy math, coming to school, not shying away from it. It's an area where a lot of times minority kids feel they can't be successful. I want them to know they can be successful at it."

She adds, "I don't seek to embarrass my kids. If they get a wrong answer, then we've got to ask, 'How did you get that answer?' Then it becomes less intimidating if they're not correct."

Toliver generally has her students work together in groups; she says they are more comfortable learning that way. And as for textbooks, well, forget it. "You'll notice that there's never a textbook even mentioned here," she says.

She favors performance-based tests over paper-and-pencil tests in evaluating her students. For one such examination, Toliver had each student form a pentagon from any combination of six pattern-block pieces: a square, an equilateral triangle, a rectangle, a trapezoid, a parallelogram, and a rhombus. The students' task was to determine the sum of the interior angles of the pentagon, and they had to explain how they got their answers. "The bottom line was, they had to go through the process, and they had to write up and explain what they did. And that was a test. And it was graded one to ten. And most of them did pretty well."

One of Toliver's most popular projects is the "Math Trail," in which students create books of real-world math problems. One such book, on display in Toliver's classroom, was put together last year by a group of students calling themselves "The Untouchables." In the book's introduction, the students wrote, "The problems in our book are comprised of things around us. Continue if you are a person who is not afraid to learn or try something new. We are trying to prove that the classroom is NOT the only place to learn math. So sit back, relax, and watch the Untouchables discover math."

The book contains a number of photographs of sites around the neighborhood, each site containing a math problem. For example, next to a photo of a house on 106th Street is this puzzler: "There are two fire escapes on the outside of the building. If one is rusted and opens twice as slowly as the other, which opens in 7.4 seconds, how long will it take the rusted one to open?"

The Math Trail book incorporates at least two of the ideas Toliver holds dear to her heart: It allows her students to "discover" that math exists all around them, and it forces them to use their writing skills in communicating the math problems they create.

Toliver also has her students keep journals; she wants to know how they feel about math and school. Once, in her seventh grade math class, Toliver sensed that her students were having difficulty understanding how to measure an isosceles triangle. "I knew they were getting frustrated," Toliver recalls, "so I asked them to tell me right then and there, 'How do you feel? What's on your mind at this moment?' And here's what some of them said." She pulls out some samples:

"I feel very puzzled but I think I have the answer to Miss Toliver's problem."

"I feel very tired because I went late to sleep last night. It affects my way of working because every time I lay on the desk."

"I feel that the room is stuffy and hot. Because of this I can't find the way to solve the problem that Miss Toliver gave me. I also feel very sleepy and hungry."

"Right now my brain is tired. I feel tired because I haven't had any sleep and my brain cells aren't energized enough."

"I feel kind of funny because I really don't know how to measure an isosceles triangle, but I'm going to try hard so I could feel great."

Toliver: "I wanted to know how they were feeling about the task. And I knew they weren't used to my teaching style. The fact is, they were being driven nuts. But I tell my students from the beginning, 'In this room, you're expected to think. And it's not going to be all spoon-fed to you. You will have to apply yourself, and you're going to discover that you know more than you really think you know.'"

"Kay has a way of bringing math alive," says special education teacher Marrero. "She has a way of making it interdisciplinary so that it's not just all numbers. It's literature, it's folklore, it's culture, it's history, and you can see the connections."

Some of Toliver's students go on to East Harlem's Manhattan Center for Science and Mathematics, while others get accepted into

New York City's more elite—and highly selective—specialized high schools, such as Stuyvesant or the Bronx High School of Science. A few students opt to pursue vocational training.

Toliver is proud of all her students, but she is especially proud of the ones who go on to college. Like her former student who will graduate from Brown University in June. Or the one at Cornell. Or the one at Syracuse University. Or the one who graduated last year from the University of Virginia.

"It's like everything else," Toliver says. "You have those who make it and those who don't. But the hope is that all of them will."

* * * * * * *

Kay Toliver would probably be a remarkable teacher in any school, but there is no doubt that East Harlem Tech has given her the opportunity to flourish as a professional. Toliver's tenure at the school (she began her career as a student teacher at P.S. 72 in 1966) is persuasive testimony to that fact.

Jack Perna, director of District 4's Professional Science Center, recently completed a dissertation on East Harlem Tech for Kansas State University. His conclusion: "It's basically a school that has a very enlightened staff."

The teachers at East Harlem Tech are lucky to have a principal, Susan Siegel, who gives them the freedom to teach the way they see fit. "We all know what we want to teach and what we like to do, and we are able to do it," one teacher told Perna. "There is no one breathing down our necks telling us what we can and cannot do. We check in with the principal to let her know what we are doing, but it is very flexible and independent. It means I run my curriculum the way I want to run it."

Siegel also gives her teachers the power to set many of the school's policies, although she has the final say. "It's decision by consensus," Perna says. "Unless everyone agrees, there's no decision. They keep working until they reach that consensus." The school's teachers meet with Siegel at least once a month to present her with ideas and to get her "seal of approval." Says one teacher, "If there is a problem, we discuss it first and then we go to administration for consent for what we want to do. And usually administration is supportive. But when decisions need to be made, it's the group together, and we move on from there. When we meet with the [principal] we have already developed a game plan. We have already decided which way we want it to go."

No one disputes that Kay Toliver is the "lead teacher" at East Harlem Tech. "Kay is the senior teacher," Perna says, "so she's looked upon by the other teachers as one of the prime movers of the school."

"She has an impact on new teachers," adds Marrero, "especially those who are very shy with math. She does staff development, and I've seen teachers who are very reticent come up to her after the session and say, 'Could you help me with this?' and she always follows up. And then they use her ideas in their classrooms. So she does have a real impact."

Principal Siegel puts it another way: "I call her a magician. Her energy just runs through this building."

In 1991, Toliver was one of twenty-two New York–area teachers selected as a Fellow for the Advancement of Mathematics Education, a three-year program administered by Long Island University. The FAME fellows meet for an entire month during the summer and once a month during the school year, returning to their schools with new ideas for their colleagues. "It's a wonderful program," Toliver says. "I think it's important that teachers in this building be very much aware of what's going on in math education because what's going on in math affects what's going on in English and affects what's going on in social studies."

* * * * * * *

Elba Marrero sounds like a proud mother when she talks about Kay Toliver, her friend and colleague. "I'm so happy for her," she gushes.

"She's just all aglow now. She's more self-assured. She's done all these great things all these years and never got any real accolades about it, and now she's getting her due."

And so, it seems, is East Harlem Tech. "This year's been wonderful," Susan Siegel says. The attention, she adds, "has done a lot for us. We're here in a tough neighborhood. Things are not getting better around us. So to know that she's one of us, and she's being acknowledged, makes everybody feel good."

Meanwhile, in Room 504, Toliver is taking a break between classes. A student enters the classroom with a Federal Express package addressed to the teacher. It is a wooden plaque from the Coca-Cola Company congratulating Toliver on being named a finalist in the Disney American Teacher Awards. It says:

"I touch the future; I teach." Christa McAuliffe
The Coca-Cola Company proudly salutes Ms. Kay Toliver
East Harlem Tech/P.S. 72 Manhattan, New York, NY
A Champion of Our Future.

Toliver is elated. "Oh, I love it," she says. "I do touch the future. I truly believe that."

David Hill

• • • • • • •

Kay Toliver was the subject of a 1993 PBS special titled Good Morning, Miss Toliver *and was honored as a "living legend" by NBC during black history month early in 1994. Still teaching at East Harlem Tech, Toliver is also the host of a PBS series on mathematics for elementary school children called* The Eddie Files.

This chapter originally appeared as an article in *Teacher Magazine*, May 1993.

9

Maine Attraction

Nancie Atwell

Down a snowy lane in Edgecomb, Maine, a town with more steeples than stoplights, the blanket of white is interrupted only by spruce trees and the occasional house with a snake of smoke escaping from the chimney. Fences of stacked, weathered rails zigzag across the frozen countryside.

Just off the road stands a two-story, clapboard structure with an addition jutting off one side. It looks like any other house, except for the bell on the roof. Inside, a sea of children are seated on pillows in a large carpeted room. Facing them, with sun pouring through three windows behind her, is a woman with thick, dark hair pulled back in a headband. Dressed in a maroon sweater that covers a flower-print blouse and a long gray-green skirt, she sits cross-legged in a rocking chair, leaning forward with elbows resting on her knee like a mother reading to her children.

The woman is Nancie Atwell, renowned teacher, author, and researcher. The building is the Center for Teaching and Learning, the K–6 private school she built with royalties from her popular book, *In the Middle*, and with her own hard work.

In the back of the bookshelf-lined room, three women furiously take notes. Teachers at Fayette Central School, a little over an hour away, the visitors do not want to miss a thing. Atwell does not want them to miss anything either; they are, after all, the main reason she built this school.

The center represents Atwell's vision for school reform in the United States: give thoughtful teachers real and practical models of good classroom practice—what she calls "primary sources"—so they can go back to their schools and be agents for change. Atwell admits it is a "slow growth" model; only a handful of teachers at a time can visit her center. But those who do are able to immerse themselves in a school that is organized very differently from their own. They can watch as students do real-life work; they can see how the children talk to each other and interact with teachers, how parents are involved, and what the tools of teaching actually look like.

Atwell's own experience has taught her to be respectful of the time one needs to change. It was a long and painstaking journey that led her to this quaint New England building. Years of reading, thinking, talking, observing, and experimenting spurred her to reshape her classroom. Then she tried to entice other teachers to reexamine their teaching. The school was born of the frustration Atwell felt when earlier efforts—speeches, workshops, and classroom demonstrations—fell short. But she believes she may have hit on a solution.

"It's the problem of trying to imagine teaching in a different way," she explains. "How do you do that when you went to traditional school for thirteen years, went to college for six more years, and then went into a school that's always been organized one way? The only way to break the lock step and mind-set is to put people into a situation that is organized completely differently. Let them learn the rhythm and incorporate it into their heartbeat."

. . . .

The only books that Nancie Atwell had easy access to as a child growing up in Clarence, New York, a semirural bedroom community near Buffalo, were a set of encyclopedias. Her parents, a mailman and a waitress, worked hard to make ends meet. "Books," she says, "were just not something people could afford."

In high school, Atwell was a tough kid who traveled with a tough crowd. "She was smart as hell but not necessarily playing the school game," says her longtime friend and well-known educator Donald Graves.

"Education was really not where my ambitions lay at all," Atwell recalls. "I just wanted to get out of high school, marry my boyfriend, live in a trailer, and party."

Her school days may not have turned her on to education, but they had an impact. "I've always found her an enormous champion for the underdog," Graves says, "for kids who have known what it is to struggle, because she has known it, too."

Atwell and her brother were the first members of their extended family to attend college, but even that was mostly by happenstance. She won a New York Regents scholarship, which would pay her way to the State University College at Buffalo. She remembers her mother saying, "This is too good to pass up. Go for a year; if you don't like it, you don't like it. At least give it a try."

She started out majoring in art, a subject she loved in high school. But after a year of taking only art courses, she realized that she missed reading and writing, so she signed up for some English classes. In the fall term of 1970, Atwell landed in a seminar taught by a professor named Toby McLeod. "It completely turned my head around," she says. "It was a course where people talked passionately about ideas that were represented in literature, argued, acted out scenes from plays, and debated. It wasn't just people flapping their gums; we had strong personal opinions that were rooted in text. I had never heard this kind of discourse, certainly never in an English class in high school."

After receiving her bachelor's degree in English, Atwell stayed around the area for another semester to get certified to teach. "Teaching was something to do until I figured out what I really wanted to do," she says.

But in the classroom, she understood for the first time what it means to have an aptitude for something. "What happened, even during my student teaching, is that I discovered I loved it," she says. "I had never done anything that I loved as much as teaching.

"It just seemed to be miraculous that you could have this kind of dialogue with kids," she adds, still with a note of incredulity in her voice. "That this would be a job and that you would be paid to do it. It gave me extraordinary pleasure." She pauses. "It still does."

Atwell says Tonawanda Middle School, where she did her student teaching and later landed a full-time job, was an extraordinary place to begin her career. At the time, her methods were mostly traditional, but her principal, "an enlightened instructional leader," expected teachers to be learners, constantly questioning their practice.

The wild beauty of the Maine coast, however, lured her away just a year and a half later. While on vacation with her new husband, Toby McLeod, the professor who brought literature to life for her, Atwell interviewed for an opening as an English teacher at Boothbay Harbor Grammar School. The superintendent of schools there asked her flat-out if she would focus on teaching grammar. She said no; she had trained to teach kids to write, and that would be her first priority. As she left, she was certain that she would not get the job.

Days before the start of the school year, Atwell got a call from the Boothbay superintendent. The other job candidate had seen the classroom where she would be teaching and backed out. The superintendent asked Atwell if she still wanted the job.

So the couple put a new muffler on their beat-up Valiant, tranquilized the dog, and headed back to Maine. The day before school was to start, Atwell saw for herself why the other candidate had jumped ship. The school building, a Civil War–era structure, should have been condemned. There were rats, and raw sewage was seeping into some of the classrooms. Her own classroom was half of a big room, separated from another class by massive sheets of plywood. The tile floor was half gone, and bare lightbulbs hung from the ceiling.

But it was in these shabby surroundings that Nancie Atwell gave birth to "thoughtfulness" in her classroom. The story of how she came out from behind her desk to sit with her students and understand better how they learn has reached more than two hundred thousand teachers through *In the Middle* (Boynton/Cook, 1987). In her book, Atwell describes how she puzzled over students' behavior, invited researchers to observe and comment on her class, and looked critically at her practice. Deep analysis of what she does when she writes spurred her to experiment with structures that would help, rather than hinder, students' writing. "I saw the choices I made as a writer—deciding how, when, what, and for whom I'd write—weren't options available to writers in my classroom," she recounts in the book.

In the process, she reached out to other teachers in her school, not with answers but with questions. With a two-year grant from the federal government, she launched the Boothbay Writing Project to study the writing process. The twenty-three teachers involved read research papers, attended professional conferences together, kept detailed logs of observations of students, and discussed their own writing.

The teachers met formally and informally. Many of the conversations took place at the Thistle Inn, a bar they frequented. "We were madly talking all of the time about what we were finding," she remembers, "thinking about how the whole system of writing instruction in the school needed to be changed based on what we were learning."

"The process worked," she writes in *In the Middle*. "It worked because it was so complex. Layer upon layer of experience accumulated to form a body of shared knowledge and expertise. No one handed us a program from on high; in intense and personally meaningful collaboration, we invented our own wheel. Together, we learned from ourselves, each other, and our students."

They created a model for a writing workshop for students that later spread throughout Boothbay Region Elementary School, the new consolidated school where they taught. Students were given regular chunks of time to write. They chose their own topics and genres and were given feedback during, not just after, the writing process. Teachers covered the mechanics of writing in short mini-lessons and when issues came up during individual writing conferences. The teachers wrote themselves and talked to students about their own writing.

Donald Graves, then a professor at the University of New Hampshire, remembers his first encounter with Atwell's eighth graders' work. "We were just amazed at what her students wrote," he says. "It wasn't just single pieces; she showed us whole collections where you could see how students first started and what they could do toward the end. I've seen very few situations where students changed so dramatically." In 1985, her students scored the second highest in Maine's writing assessment; a fifth of her students were in the ninety-ninth percentile.

Atwell soon began to wonder how all she had learned about writing applied to her reading program. Her talks with Toby around the dinner table became the yardstick by which she measured her reading class. "It is a literate environment," she says of her dinner table in *In the Middle*. "Around it, people talk in all the ways literate people discourse. We don't need assignments, lesson plans, teacher's manuals, or handbooks. We need only another literate person. And our talk isn't sterile or grudging or perfunctory. It's filled with jokes, arguments, exchanges of bits of information, descriptions of what we loved and hated and why. The way Toby and I chat most evenings at that table were ways that my kids and I could chat, entering literature together. Somehow, I had to get that table into my classroom and invite my eighth graders to pull up their chairs."

The "table" she developed for her classroom was the reading workshop. The idea behind it was that students learn to read by reading. She let students choose what to read just as real readers do and gave them opportunities to discuss what they were reading. Atwell flooded her room with books—both recognized literature and popular novels, such as S. E. Hinton's *The Outsiders*. She required students to read all period long and regularly write letters about what they were reading to her and other students. Students who had never voluntarily read a book were reading an average of thirty-five a year.

Throughout *In the Middle*, Nancie Atwell shows in painstaking detail that thoughtful change happens only through careful observation of how kids learn to read and write. She became an avid data collector. Her students' writing stayed in school all year; she scoured the material, looking for growth and changes. Every day, she filled out a "status of the class" chart, so she could look for patterns over time. She did some number crunching, keeping track of how many books students read and what genres were represented, what punctuation they used in writing, and what students chose to write about and why. She even interviewed her students about their own learning. "My experience as a teacher who observed her students—as a teacher-researcher—has changed me forever. Everywhere I look I see data," Atwell writes in a later book, *Side by Side*. "As I filled my notebooks, my teaching became more patient and more sensible."

Still, she needed a structure for all this information. "*In the Middle* became a story of me and my students and our struggles to make sense of school," she writes, "and I became the rueful, insightful, cheerful first person that my husband sometimes wishes he were married to when he finishes reading a manuscript with my name on it."

In the Middle, which struck a chord among teachers because it presents teaching as an intellectual activity but in a practical way, won her a loyal following and critical acclaim. She was the first classroom teacher to receive the David H. Russell Award for outstanding research in the teaching of English from the National Council of Teachers of English and the prestigious Mina P. Shaughnessy Prize from the Modern Language Association.

The awards were a welcome affirmation but did not really change how she felt about herself and her work. "I have such an ego," she says with a self-deprecating laugh, "that I really believed

I had something to say." Still, the attention was not for naught. She believes that the recognition she received lends credibility to other teachers who want to conduct research in their own classrooms.

The acclaim also made her a hot commodity on the lecture and consulting circuit. Atwell had left the Boothbay school system after her daughter was born in 1986, the year before *In the Middle* was published. Over the next few years, she conducted independent research and directed a writing-across-the-curriculum project for elementary schools through the Breadloaf School of English in Middlebury, Vermont. But between 1987 and 1990, she also accepted more than thirty speaking engagements. She welcomed the opportunities, hoping she would be able to reach other teachers with her discoveries and challenge them to reenvision their classrooms.

She found the process of writing speeches rewarding; it forced her again to sit down and think about what went on in her classroom. "I've never written anything where I wasn't surprised in the act of writing," she says. "I'm always amazed by what turns up." She remembers one speech-writing epiphany in particular. She was writing about two very different students who had been lagging but gradually became successful in her class. "I can remember almost falling off my chair when, as I was sitting there with my data in my dining room, I figured out what was going on with these two kids," she says. "There is no other feeling like that, finding the connection and then trying to find the language for it before you lose it." Many of these speeches later evolved into articles for publication.

Although she enjoyed preparing the speeches, Atwell found that giving them was not a very effective way to reach teachers. She felt like "a talking head." And delivering them, she remembers, was often a letdown. "The unfortunate thing about speaking is that the learning part was over by the time I left my house," she says. "Then I had to go deliver the speech. By then, it was dead on the page."

She was further dismayed to see that a kind of cult movement had formed around her work. After giving a speech, she would find herself hounded by teachers, who said things like, "Your book is my bible, and you're my guide."

"It's one thing to have people say in a letter, 'I admire your work,' but it's another for people to take work that is serious and intellectual and turn it into a charismatic movement," she says. *In the Middle* offers a model of a teacher who found her own problems and used every resource available, especially her own students, to solve the problems. I want teachers to be professional enough to respect the genesis of the story."

Traveling around the country, leading teachers in in-service training, Atwell saw some other trends that disturbed her. "Everywhere I went, I would be sandwiched between the Madeline Hunter person and the thinking-skills person," she says. The programs these people were touting seemed to force artificial frameworks on teaching and learning and missed the crux of the problem and the solution: the relationship between teacher and student. "There was always some obstacle between us and kids, some prism through which you have to look at kids, something that will make teaching more efficient, easier, cleaner, neater, less emotional."

To break through this barrier, Atwell began looking for opportunities to teach teachers in situations where they could witness and experience a different kind of interaction between teacher and students. In graduate courses she taught through Northeastern University, she ran half of each class as a writing workshop, treating the student-teachers like her eighth graders, so they could feel how it worked. And she took up demonstration teaching, where she would take on a class and invite other teachers to observe. Atwell's friend Donald Graves watched her teach a class of students in Atlanta that she had never seen before. "She has that knack of making almost instant contact at a student's level," he says. "She doesn't do it by coming down to the student. She is able to produce this incredible invitation to the student to go where she is going."

Atwell recalls those experiences with mixed feelings. "That was closer to what I wanted because at least teachers could see it happening with real kids," she says. "But in some ways it was still artificial because they weren't my students. I had no idea what had happened before I came in; I had no idea what was going to happen after. So the context was strange."

Atwell was ready for the next step. She wanted to continue teaching and working with teachers, but she wanted to do it right, without staying in a Holiday Inn every weekend. She also wanted to remain in Maine, an area that she and her husband love. And she needed a place for her daughter, Anne, to go to school.

So on August 2, 1990, a grueling year after Atwell decided to start her own school, builders broke ground on the Center for Teaching and Learning in nearby Edgecomb. By August 29, they had fit together two pieces of the prefab house and secured the roof. On September 10, Nancie Atwell cried; the movers had brought the furniture, and, for the first time, the center looked like a real school. On September 12, she and two other teachers—Donna Maxim and Susan Stires—opened their doors to thirty students.

* * * * * * *

In a part of the country that is run by town meetings, the students at the Center for Teaching and Learning have a distinct advantage: they are learning to speak out. When they are taken on field trips, the guide inevitably asks, "Who are these kids?" It's not because they are brilliant or particularly articulate; it is because they have a voice. They ask questions and want to know things.

One reason is that the school day starts and ends with a meeting attended by all fifty-eight students, kindergartners to sixth graders, who sit side by side with their teachers in one room. On this bright winter's morning, Nancie Atwell leads the group from her rocking chair, peppering the talk with Spanish phrases the students have learned.

The meeting starts simply enough, with children raising hands to tell their news from the weekend. One describes a ride on a snowmobile sled; another tells how she spotted a fox. Atwell asks if anyone has heard any national news. "Arthur Ashe died of AIDS," one offers. Teachers and students alike talk about who this man was, the disease, and the loss.

Then Atwell leads them in reciting a poem; students clap and snap their fingers in rhythm. After that, Atwell reads aloud an excerpt from an interview with Eloise Greenfield, a poet they have read. According to the article, Greenfield does her best writing from about midnight to 4 A.M. The children gasp. Greenfield's advice to young writers: If you read a book you like, read it again to see how the author puts the words together.

Atwell then reads from a book about the Underground Railroad, and the group discusses it. Following the discussion, the students sing a song that they wrote about the work of the school.

This rich exchange takes about fifteen minutes.

The only people who remain silent through the meeting are the three teachers from Fayette Central School. One of eight teams of teachers invited to spend a week at the school this year, the "interns" are asked not to speak to the children or teachers during class. This way, Atwell says, they can concentrate on observing and reflecting without interfering with the dynamics of the school. In fact, to minimize the disruption, no other visitors are allowed in the school.

"The great thing about the center is that these are real kids in a real school," Atwell explains. "We have a stake in what happens to them."

The interns are encouraged to take detailed notes and jot down questions to ask the teachers during meetings that are scheduled throughout their stay. As the week progresses, these women sometimes sit shoulder to shoulder with a teacher as she confers with a student; they scrawl notes but say nothing.

The application process for the intern program is rigorous. The teachers in each team must write essays about their professional development and their educational philosophy. The team application must include a letter from the school administrator stating that the teachers will be allowed to make changes based on what they learn during the visit. Each team leaves at the end of the week with a long- and short-term plan and three graduate credits.

When the morning meeting adjourns, most of the students scramble off to their work; a few stay behind to put the pillows back into an oversized closet.

Unlike at most schools, the students at the center do not have assigned desks. Instead, they move among four major rooms: the reading room, writing room, math and science room, and projects room. The rooms are plentifully stocked with the tools that real readers, writers, scientists, mathematicians, and artists would use. Students are broken into four groups by grade levels—kindergarten, 1–2, 3–4, 5–6—so most students stay with the same teacher for two years.

This morning, Atwell joins teacher Susan Benedict and her fifth and sixth graders in the writing room, an open space with wooden tables of different sizes to accommodate different-size children. Strategically placed around the room are folders, papers, pencils, pens, scissors, books on writing, a dictionary, and a thesaurus. Atwell joins the students in a circle of chairs. A quotation by the poet Rainer Maria Rilke posted on the wall behind her captures the essence of the minilesson Atwell is about to teach: "Be patient toward all that is unsolved in your heart, and try to love the questions themselves."

Atwell tells them about an experience her friend Donald Graves had recently on a flight to Atlanta. Graves found himself sitting next to someone from Boothbay, a man named Barry Sherman, whose twenty-three-year-old son, B.J., had died in a car accident a few weeks earlier. Graves asked Sherman if he knew Nancie Atwell. "Yes," he replied, "She was the best teacher B.J. ever had." Sherman went on to tell Graves how he cherishes the piece of B.J.'s writing that Atwell excerpted in her book. When he reads it, Sherman says, he can hear B.J.'s voice and understand his feelings.

Atwell hands out copies of B.J.'s story about moving out of his mother's house to live with his dad. "We've been talking about narrative voice," she says. "This is in the third person. I call this fiction. Some of it is real; some is made-up."

As she reads aloud, the students follow along, gripped by the tale. She finishes, and, after a long period of silence, she asks quietly, "Why did Barry Sherman remember this piece of writing?"

"Because it was an important incident," one student offers.

"Because B.J. was trying to work out his feelings in it," another adds.

Atwell lets other ideas emerge before she adds her own: "Because it was something that mattered to B.J. I call it authentic fiction. These are the things that last. When you sit down to write, ask yourself: Is it a real need I have? Is there some tension or problem I want to work out? Otherwise, all you're doing is an exercise to fill time."

She ends with a quotation from playwright Neil Simon: "I can't write anything unless my character wants something dearly."

Although Atwell does not have a class of her own in the center, she thinks of herself as the instructional leader. When Atwell and Benedict noticed that students in Benedict's class were turning out a lot of beautiful but voiceless writing, Atwell offered to teach a series of minilessons on the purpose of writing. Teacher Donna Maxim, who knows Atwell from Boothbay Writing Project days, says, "To watch her do a minilesson is one of the greatest pleasures in my life. She's such a great writer, and she can just talk to kids and make them aspire to be great writers, too."

As the writer's workshop continues, the students move off to tables to work. Some meet with Benedict for a writing conference during which they pose questions about their work in progress, read the piece aloud, and ask for comments and suggestions.

(Even the kindergartners at the center learn this process. For example, they have written a parody of the popular children's book *Bread and Jam for Francis*, a piece called "Bagels and Salsa for Nancy," about how their teacher eats bagels and salsa for lunch every day.)

Later in the day, Benedict's students gather, sprawled comfortably on the floor of the reading room, to hear her read aloud from *Roll of Thunder, Hear My Cry,* a book by Mildred Taylor set in the 1930s. In the chapter, a black man who has gone into town with his son is attacked by white men on his way home. After the reading, Benedict asks the students what they think. The conversation that ensues is easygoing but firmly rooted in the text.

"She describes too much . . . that part about the cracking bones," one girl says with a shudder.

"I predict Papa's going to die," a boy adds.

"What does Mildred Taylor care about?" asks the teacher.

After a moment, Curt, who is reclined on the floor, says, "She wants to tell us what really went on at that time, to really feel it. Not like the history books. She wants to show us the human side of history."

Nathaniel, obviously troubled by the events in the book, asks, "Could a white person get arrested for shooting a black person?"

In virtual unison, the kids say, "No. Now, but not back then."

Kristin expounds on the idea: "I think she's against racism. She's showing how wrong it is for a white person to shoot a black person."

Benedict pushes: "Is she promoting integration?"

When the students answer no, she asks, "What in the book leads you to believe that?"

They point out that the blacks and whites in the book live separately and that one of the most prominent characters, a black gentleman whom readers grow to respect, is against his son's becoming friends with a white boy.

All of the students at the center spend half an hour to an hour reading independently each day, but there is also ample opportunity to hear good literature read aloud. Like most teaching at the center, the decision to read aloud to the students was based on research. It has been shown, Atwell points out, that listening to someone read builds students' long-term memory. "Reading aloud isn't just charming," Maxim tells one of the Fayette teachers. "It is essential."

* * * * * * *

Since the opening of the Center for Teaching and Learning, the dinner-table talk at the Atwell-McLeod house has not been confined to books. Recently, their daughter, Anne, who is now a first grader at the center, cleared off a space at the table after dinner to draw electronic circuits in series and in parallel on paper napkins. She wondered which kind of circuit would conduct more power. Anne was still thinking about her science class, where she had learned about circuits by making them. Students at the center investigate science as real scientists do, by asking real questions and setting up small experiments to prove or disprove a theory.

Recently, when teachers at the center talked about how they were going to have children write formally about the work they were doing in science, Atwell dug up a series of papers that a rain forest biologist who visited the school had presented at a scholarly conference. The teachers studied them and decided to use them as a model.

Today, in keeping with this real-world philosophy, Donna Maxim starts a conversation about magnets with her third and fourth graders by passing out magnets and asking students what they know about them. On a piece of chart paper, she writes their ideas: "Magnets attract and repel." "They have poles."

A student named Meghan interrupts with a question: "Do magnets attract all metals?" Maxim writes down Meghan's question (it is, after all, the point of the lesson) and asks her what made her think of it. Meghan explains that she has a butterfly magnet at home that does not stick to all surfaces.

Maxim hands a nail to each student and poses a question: "What will happen to the nail if it is kept near the magnet for a while?" The students think out loud: "It will make the nail lighter?" "It will make it rust?" "The magnet will 'magnetify' the nail."

"Is a nail a magnet?" Maxim asks. Most of the students say no, but one boy says yes. Maxim asks him, "Will this nail pick up a paper clip like our magnet?" The boy says no.

"Is it a magnet?" she pushes.

The boy does not budge; he says yes. Another student postulates that maybe all things are magnets but in different degrees. With that, the class launches into a discussion about electricity, conductors, and insulators—all aspects of one of the school's themes this year, energy.

It is just this kind of rigorous exchange that Patricia Dickinson, one of the teachers from Fayette Central School, says really shakes up her thinking. "Everything they do is a meaningful learning experience for the children," she says. "They never ask the students to do anything unless it is authentic and has a reason. This is something I will think about constantly now. Is this really an authentic activity? Could I make it more so? How could I do it?"

The center's teachers and the interns probe the issues surrounding thoughtful teaching in a series of meetings, often held in the teachers' upstairs office. (The space is comfortable. The teachers each have their own desks, but they are grouped together to promote collegiality.) They first discuss some of the surface details the interns have noticed about the school. The way teachers and students remove their shoes when they enter the building, so the floors stay clean enough for students to sit and lie on. The way there are no chalkboards so there is less dust. The way students call their teachers by their first names so they realize the teachers are real people.

Then the talk turns to bigger issues. How to create a rigorous intellectual atmosphere in which students still feel safe enough to take risks. How to give students real choices in a structured way. As they get into the nitty-gritty, the teachers quote liberally from research on teaching and from reading they have done in the subject areas.

As the week draws to a close, the conversation at these meetings focuses on the most pressing issue: how will these three teachers be able to go back to their public school and create a more thoughtful learning environment? Although their classrooms are housed in a trailer, the Fayette teachers hope to create a kind of ghetto for real learning next year. Among other things, they decide to meet weekly to talk about their practice, make presentations to parents and administrators about their experience and ideas, begin reshaping their classes, and work to get doors installed between their classrooms.

But Atwell insists that this group will go away with something even more important. "They began to understand that they could be brave together," she says, "that there was real power in the coherence of their theory. There was a new sense of what was possible when teachers who shared beliefs got together and tried to forge some common ground."

· · · · · · ·

Nancie Atwell calls the time she spent preparing to open the Center for Teaching and Learning "the nightmare part" of her life. When she went looking for a place to house the school, the first three sites fell through. Her decision to build a new school gave her more control over its layout but also filled the following months with hundreds of details she had to work out. Even after the land was purchased and a blueprint drafted, it took four months to get approval from the local planning board. The application was roughly a hundred pages long and cost more than $4,000 to compile.

"I have never worked so hard, so long, so consistently on anything in my life," she says. "They were eighteen-hour days—developing the plan, walking the site, taking measurements, digging holes, and meeting with groups of people about one thing or another."

Fundraising was an enormous chore. Atwell knew that her teaching model would not hold water if she served only the typical private school clientele. To make sure her students represented the socioeconomic profile of rural Maine, she wanted to offer generous scholarships to offset the $3,350 tuition. So she sent a mass mailing to teachers she had come into contact with over the years, asking for donations. (She now receives about $10,000 a year in checks, ranging from $10 to $100.)

But she still needed more money to build the school. "It's been awful, the most humbling experience in my life," she says of her fundraising effort. "I think I have this great professional reputation, and I go to foundations, and they have never heard of Nancie Atwell, they have never heard of In the Middle, and, after I explain my model for changing schools, they tell me they won't fund a local project."

Despite grants from the Bingham Trust, the Betterment Fund, and the New York Times Foundation and a $50,000 no-strings-attached donation from veteran actor James Whitmore, she still had to collect her pension from Maine's teacher retirement fund to make a down payment on a mortgage. Some of her royalties from In the Middle go directly to the school. So far, she has received no pay from the center. Her husband keeps asking, half-jokingly, when she is going to draw a salary.

Despite her fiscal precariousness, Atwell is ready for a new challenge. She plans to open a secondary school soon. "If the model we have for the elementary school is powerful," she says, "the next level of work is going to be absolutely groundbreaking."

Others agree. Secondary education is her area of expertise, and there is a real paucity of models out there for middle and high school teachers. No matter what Nancie Atwell is doing, Donald Graves says, she provides a powerful example for others. "She expects so much of herself," he says, "that to hang around her you start to think, 'My God, am I carrying my weight?' She's not demanding that you do it, but you want to join her professionally."

The tough question is whether others can really follow in Atwell's footsteps. "You can't bypass the fact that she is one hell of a reader, writer, thinker, and learner," Graves says. "On the other hand, there are lots of teachers out there who are on the verge and who just need the chance to see a real pro at work."

Elizabeth Schulz

• • • • • • •

In September 1994, the Center for Teaching and Learning will open its doors for the first time to seventh and eighth graders. Nancie Atwell plans to give up some of her administrative duties to teach reading, writing, and history in the new middle school.

♦ ♦ ♦ ♦ ♦ ♦ ♦

David B. Sutton

This chapter originally appeared as an article in *Teacher Magazine*, August 1993.

10

• •

Woman on a Mission
Lynn Cherkasky-Davis

In 1979, at age thirty, veteran Chicago kindergarten teacher Lynn Cherkasky-Davis began to suffer the symptoms of burnout. Teaching, once her life's passion, now had all the allure of a monotonous clock-punching job. She arrived at school at 8:30 A.M. At 2:30 P.M., after the last bell had rung, she fled the building. Perhaps, she considered, ten years of teaching in an urban school had simply taken their inevitable toll; perhaps a change of scenery was all she needed. Driving home through blocks of empty lots and the rubble of razed buildings, she sometimes thought about teaching in the suburbs, where the salaries were higher, the schools calmer, and the neighborhoods as green and safe as they had been in her hometown of Kaukauna, Wisconsin.

About her own teaching career, she felt as she had about her recently failed marriage: that she was blowing it, that something she could not quite figure out had gone awry. Of course, she could not discuss her doubts with her principal or fellow teachers; to do so was impolitic at best, a sign of flagrant weakness at worst. Like the other teachers, she kept her classroom door closed; what went on behind that door was no one else's business.

The strange thing was that, by all conventional measures, Cherkasky-Davis was successful. Her students performed well on worksheets and standardized tests, such as the Metropolitan Reading Readiness Test. And she was well organized, too. If she planned to have her students on page 13 of their workbooks by Tuesday, then she would make sure they were there, no matter what. Why, then, did she feel her teaching was less than adequate? She could not say.

Then one day, a seemingly minor misunderstanding led to what she would later call an epiphany. She asked an African-American child to please bring her a pen. "A what?" the boy asked. "A pen." "What for?" "A note for your mother," Cherkasky-Davis said. The boy, knowing that his teacher often pinned notes for home to the back of her students' shirts, went to her desk and brought back a safety pin. "I asked for a pen," she said with some irritation. "A *pen*." The boy looked bewildered, and, suddenly, Cherkasky-Davis had the crucial insight: he could not distinguish between those words with short *e*'s and those with short *i*'s, even though he, like most of his classmates, could do so on standardized tests that required students to match pictured objects with given vowel sounds. The problem, she came to realize, was that knowing enough to circle the right answers on a test did not translate into authentic knowledge; mastering an isolated skill was no guarantee that the skill could be called upon in everyday life.

From that day forward, Cherkasky-Davis could no longer see children as vases to be filled with phonic and spelling rules in the hope that they would somehow be transformed into readers and writers. She began a long journey away from traditional teaching, grounded in basals and drilling, toward a holistic approach that integrated reading, writing, and math. It was a journey that would bring her in contact with teachers who shared her frustrations and hopes, the kind of teachers who would eventually help her in 1992 start the Foundations School—the first public school in Chicago devised and operated by teachers.

* * * * * * *

Cherkasky-Davis speaks frequently of the importance of teachers acquiring "voice," and it is apparent at a Monday morning faculty meeting that the Foundations School teachers have voice—if voice means speaking one's mind without concern for undue diplomatic caution. Disagreement over issues is expressed with both stridency and occasional profanity. The subject that arouses the most ire this morning is lesson plans. Carl Lawson, the principal of Price School, which houses Foundations (Foundations is a school within a school), has asked the teachers to submit them.

"He's welcome to come into our classrooms to see what the hell we're doing," one teacher says. "But we're not going to make up any lesson plans."

"I feel that we ought to try to accommodate him on this one," Cherkasky-Davis says. "Thanks to him, your third graders don't have to take the Iowa [Test of Basic Skills], and he's going to take shit for that."

But the other teachers appear unanimous in their resistance to turning in lesson plans. To them, it represents Big Brother authoritarianism, the kind of administrative fiat that, in part, drove them to start their own school. In contrast to other public schools, Foundations School is a democracy; the teachers make decisions as equal partners. While Cherkasky-Davis is the school's leader and facilitator—a kind of unofficial principal—she does not pass on mandates to the other teachers. In fact, upon joining Foundations, each teacher agreed that he or she would resign if the others felt that his or her classroom work was less than superior.

Furthermore, the teachers are philosophically opposed to formal lesson plans as dangerously constrictive. Learning, Foundations teachers believe, means not dictating to students but rather guiding them on a path of their own choosing; discovery, the essence of learning, cannot be charted in advance.

The meeting breaks up indeterminately, and, afterward, Cherkasky-Davis is somewhat piqued with her colleagues. "To hand Dr. Lawson lesson plans is bullshit, a fictionalized account of what we're going to do; in the classroom, we have to go with the flow," she says. "But he's always supported us—he's the one who's enabled us to be here—so my feeling is, let's do our lesson plans; let's give him what he needs. But the teachers are thinking, 'We're so autonomous that we don't have to answer to daddy'—that sort of thing."

Her conciliatory stance on the lesson plan issue is unusual, for Cherkasky-Davis, a short, dark-haired woman bursting with nervous energy, has built her tough reputation partially on her general unwillingness to compromise. ("She blows the top off of a system dominated by false politeness," one acquaintance says.) For the most part, she believes that to compromise on key issues (to permit, for instance, intrusive standardized testing) is to undermine the integrity of the program. But she knows it is vital for her to be on good terms with Lawson, who, as principal of Price, also has certain administrative responsibilities for the Foundations School.

Later in the morning, Cherkasky-Davis calls on the principal and informs him of the teachers' reluctance to submit lesson plans. Lawson, a cheerful man, perhaps in his mid forties, is absolutely unfazed. "If I as a principal had to write a lesson plan, I wouldn't do it," he says, laughing. "I'd quit." Then, perhaps thinking over the teachers' resistance, he comes up with an intriguing analogy. The Foundations teachers, he suggests, are like the early dissenters of the Protestant Reformation, boldly disputing the authority of the established church.

The more one thinks about the history and philosophy of the Foundations School, the more apt Lawson's analogy seems. Unabashed iconoclasts, the Foundations teachers seem to take an almost impish glee in ruffling the feathers of the educational establishment. "We left a trail," Foundations teacher Doris Clark says of their reform efforts at Alexander Dumas School, where all of them previously worked. "It pissed off [Dumas teachers and administrators] when we made it work. And they didn't like the fact that we weren't docile and didn't allow the children to be docile either." Another teacher, Danielle Norman, says she and her reform-minded colleagues endured heavy-handed intimidation tactics from the more traditional teachers. "If I was out of the building during the day for any reason, this one teacher would have the janitor open my room to kids roaming the halls. You can imagine what happened; I was vandalized three times. We were a huge threat, empowering ourselves and others."

Lawson's analogy is also apt in that the school has a strong anti-hierarchical disposition; indeed, the faculty is dedicated to erasing certain distinctions among administrators, teachers, parents, and even students. Most students and teachers are on a first-name basis. Furthermore, parent volunteers roam freely about the classrooms, working with the children. "Many administrators," Cherkasky-Davis says, "see parents as ignorant, but I see them as the primary teachers. Of course, they criticize us sometimes, but that's no problem if you see yourself as a learner. Either I'll learn from them, or I'll explain to them why I'm doing something. Often, they'll have a good point."

◆ ◆ ◆ ◆ ◆ ◆

If Cherkasky-Davis has done things to upset the educational establishment—such as refusing to use textbooks or bringing classroom commotion into school hallways—it was far from her intention to be anything but "traditional" when she first became a teacher. A theater student at Northwestern University (not surprising considering her natural flamboyance), she traveled after graduation in 1971 to Amsterdam, where she performed in USO shows and met her former husband, a jazz musician. The daughter of a demanding surgeon, she had high ambitions as an actress but soon found herself repeatedly passed over for major roles. Unwilling to settle for a "cameo career," she applied for and received a preschool teaching position at an American school in Würzburg, West Germany. Immediately, she found herself loving both teaching and children. She also made a quick discovery: no lesson plan, regardless of how well it was conceived, could last for more than six minutes.

Returning in 1973 to Chicago, she worked at a nursery school while studying for a master's degree in early childhood education. After receiving her degree, she taught kindergarten at Robinson Elementary and then Fuller Elementary, both urban schools with largely African-American populations. While she had increasing doubts about her effectiveness as a teacher, she remained, partially through sheer inertia, a traditional teacher, making regular use of basals, worksheets, and drills. Like many other teachers, she wanted to believe that good practice was simply a matter of screaming louder, of pounding knowledge into her students' heads. But then, during her burnout phase in the late 1970s, she eventually came to realize that she would have to radically change the way she taught if she wanted to remain in the profession; to do otherwise, to continue to accommodate herself to a status quo she now considered ineffective, would be sheer hypocrisy.

Self-reliance is a major theme with Cherkasky-Davis, who has little sympathy for teachers who wait for others to improve their lot. In the educational arena, she says, there is no white knight. To think there is, is to place oneself in a very passive, subordinate role. "Lynn makes you know that if you stay with what's not working," one of her closest teacher friends says, "then you're simply not the professional you claim you are. You have an obligation to step out and do something different, even if it means receiving low ratings from your principal."

In any case, Cherkasky-Davis decided to fight the burnout syndrome by educating herself, searching for ways that would make learning more meaningful for herself and others. She also became involved with the Illinois Writing Project through the University of Illinois, Chicago, coming to understand that writing was not, as she had always believed, a rather remote, arcane craft but something accessible to herself and others. Even very young children, she realized, could write stories or at least purposefully scribble as a kind of emergent literacy. (To demonstrate what she means by "purposeful," she points to a sheet of what appears to be scribbling and notes that the "writing" moves from left to right, top to bottom.) Soon, much to her principal's chagrin, she was discarding the basals and presenting her children with authentic literature.

Although Cherkasky-Davis could see that her students were making genuine academic progress, as opposed to the specious progress recorded on standardized tests, she began to feel that merely revitalizing her own classroom teaching was not enough. Changing classroom life on an individual by individual basis was an interminable process; if broader-based change were ever to occur in Chicago's classrooms, the effort must be collective and teacher driven. It must be political as well as pedagogical and philosophical.

But many things worked against such an effort. Teachers, Cherkasky-Davis knew, were typically isolated in the classrooms. They were also extremely tentative, fearful of administrative reprisal. If teachers were to catalyze change, they must find a "voice."

When Cherkasky-Davis uses the word *voice* (she frequently begins sentences with "When I found my teacher's voice . . ."), it seems to have multiple meanings. On one level, it means discovering what one really thinks and believes, no easy matter in a rather paternalistic educational system that expects the teacher to abide by the counsel of everyone from textbook publishers to zealous reformers. On another level, the most literal level, finding one's voice means a refusal to keep silent. Once teachers have confidence in what they think, they must speak out, even if it means occasional uncomfortable confrontations.

Finally, finding one's voice means sharing what one has learned with other teachers; teachers must emerge from their often self-imposed isolation.

Cherkasky-Davis first began to find her voice in the then newly formed Chicago chapter of Teachers Applying Whole Language (TAWL). What appealed to Cherkasky-Davis most about whole language was that it was a movement rather than another series of techniques. Whole language, because it assumes that children have an intrinsic interest in and capacity to learn from a wide range of literature, showed her that she did not have to force-feed her students work sheets and drills. She could set them free, allow them to pursue that which they found naturally fascinating. As time went on, a critical nucleus of teachers in TAWL began to move from school to school, many finally ending up at Alexander Dumas. ("We chose to be together," Cherkasky-Davis says.)

At Dumas, ostracized by teachers who disapproved of whole language and their holistic perspective, they formed another group, which they dubbed "Teachers Talk." Initially meeting in restaurants and bars, the group's early sessions, Cherkasky-Davis remembers, were cathartic and therapeutic. "We had been isolated and frustrated for so long," she says, "that we'd cry, bitch, and complain. We had an open agenda and could talk about anything." But over a period of weeks and months, the nature and setting of the meetings changed. Held each Wednesday after school in rotating classrooms, Teachers Talk moved away from complaining and crying toward a more specific professional focus. Topics included assessment, literature, process writing, and so on.

The time Cherkasky-Davis's group of teachers spent at Dumas was far from agreeable. Most were recruited in 1989–90 by the school's former principal, Sylvia Peters, who made a serious tactical error when introducing the new teachers to the others. Reports vary, but according to Danielle Norman, Peters said something like, "This group of new teachers is going to turn everything around. You will model them. You have three years to make changes or to get out." The veteran Dumas teachers, largely traditionalists in their classroom approaches, resented the new teachers; they considered them intruders. The fact that most of the veterans were African-American and the new ones white did not help. The split, some observers say, acquired an unfortunate racial dimension.

But perhaps the greatest reason for the division between the two groups involved the issue of discipline. For the veteran teachers, discipline was at the heart of effective schooling; it meant order, control, teaching students the importance of obedience. "Many African-American teachers," Cherkasky-Davis says, "feel children need more discipline. They've been enculturated that way. That's how I taught for the first eight years of my career. We say, 'Our kids are failing, so let's do it louder, stronger.' But it doesn't work."

The newer teachers, on the other hand, felt that discipline, construed as order and control, was usually for the teacher's benefit, not the students'. While the new teachers occasionally envied the silence of those orderly classrooms, they also felt that the students, typically hunched over worksheets, learned little but a sullen obedience. Of course, children must treat their teachers and one another with mutual respect, but this, they believed, had little to do with overt classroom control. Their classrooms, these teachers freely acknowledge, were noisy, even chaotic, places; the holistic approach, after all, demanded that students have a great deal of latitude to explore and that teachers, particularly of the younger children, understand that work is related to play.

To the veteran teachers this was anarchy. Doris Clark, who taught at Dumas for more than twenty years before becoming a Foundations teacher, says, "They felt we weren't disciplining appropriately because we weren't punishing them. The perception was that our children weren't as quiet and subdued as they would want them to be. I was in that school for over twenty years and went through a whole metamorphosis of not hitting kids, hitting kids, and not hitting kids. I remember when I first came to Dumas, a kid was beaten with a yardstick and dragged down the hall. Some kids are extremely angry about the humiliation they've endured."

Peters left Dumas in 1992, and assistant principal Charlotte Grey, who wanted to install a "back to basics" program, became the acting principal. Having lost their chief supporter, Cherkasky-Davis's group of teachers made a radical decision: they would create their own school, preferably a school within a school at Dumas. It would be a "choice" school so that the parents would be committed to the program's philosophy. They sent a proposal to the Quest Center, an offshoot of the Chicago Teachers Union that funded teachers with innovative projects. But there were difficulties from the beginning. For one thing, they needed an endorsement from the principal. "Charlotte Grey wouldn't even read our proposal, much less sign it," Cherkasky-Davis claims. "So we sent the proposal back to Quest without the required signature and said, 'Look at your mission statement. It talks about breaking the mold, transforming classrooms. Now, put your money where your mouth is. Help us find another place to move.' Because we were the number one proposal, they said they'd support us if we could find a home for our new school."

This was but one hurdle. For while the teachers won the quick backing of the Board of Education, Ted Kimbrough, then superintendent of the Chicago schools, was less than enthusiastic about a group of gadfly teachers starting their own school. He could not justify spending money on a new school, especially when he was closing older ones. In the end, however, Kimbrough, like the officials at the Quest Center, said he would support the teachers if they could find a home for their new school. They had but twenty-four hours to do so; it was June 24, and they needed to get on the board's agenda for a meeting the following day. Only half in jest, Cherkasky-Davis talked of getting a job in Marshall Field's lingerie department.

With only hours remaining, Cherkasky-Davis and several of her supporters drove to the district's offices, where she buttonholed Lawson. He said his Price School could provide the Foundations School with ten rooms. In three hours, details were hammered out with Lawson and the local school council, Price's governing body. Cherkasky-Davis made it to the board meeting with one hour to spare, but there was yet another obstacle. Kimbrough said she had not given the board the twenty-four-hour notice required by the Open Schools Meeting Law. The board was not scheduled to meet again for a month. Then, fate intervened. The board failed to finish its business and had to reconvene in two days, which gave Cherkasky-Davis a chance to get her new school on the agenda. At that meeting, the teachers received the board's stamp of approval, and, on June 30, 1992, Foundations School officially came into existence.

· · · · · · · ·

On a hot, humid day, made even hotter because the windows in Cherkasky-Davis's kindergarten classroom—a former storeroom from which lead and asbestos had to be removed—are painted shut, the children begin the morning, as they do every morning, by reading books they have selected. They are noisy but, for the most part, reading—actually reading with lips moving, not just glancing through the pictures. Some, having obviously read their books before, "read" from memory, recognizing specific words and sentences or understanding them in the illustrative context. Others, when stuck, make an attempt to sound words out; in fact, Cherkasky-Davis occasionally aids them in their attempt. This seems surprising, for whole-language teachers are generally regarded as purists who would never deign to sound out a word. But Cherkasky-Davis insists that phonics must be integrated into whole language. "People think there's a fight between phonics and whole language, but there isn't," she says. "Whole language, after all, is about the whole thing. So I teach strategies that will help them read. If the kid's strategy is to sound out words, that's OK. What we do must come from the child if it is to be meaningful."

Indeed, following rather than directing the child is at the heart of the Foundations School's holistic philosophy. The idea is to make each child responsible for his or her learning; should the student breach that responsibility, privileges may be withdrawn. At the morning's Community Circle, for instance, the children essentially plan the day's schedule, sequencing index cards with events such as "Story Time" and "Discovery Time" printed on them. This completed, Cherkasky-Davis then says they need to talk about what happened during the last Discovery Time. Without prompting, one student says, "It was a mess." Another adds, "It was trashed." Cherkasky-Davis tells the students that on account of the trouble, certain restrictions will be in force during today's Discovery Time.

During Community Circle, the children argue about various issues, and, for the most part, Cherkasky-Davis lets them sort things out. When the discussion gets out of control, however, she tells a frustrated child to ask another child for something she needs. "I need your attention and respect," the girl says to the other. This is a phrase that will be repeated, by both teacher and students, perhaps three dozen times during the course of the day.

Discovery Time, which the children clearly love, gives the students an opportunity to visit any of a variety of stations, such as the family living station (which has a model kitchen), transportation station (trucks, trains, airplanes, etc.), manipulative station (blocks and the like), and publishing station (markers, paper, masking tape). On Monday, perhaps because of the presence of a visitor and the heat, Discovery Time was rather chaotic. But today, Tuesday, everything is drastically different. The classroom is noisy, but the children are extremely well focused; the mood is of a busy and productive office. Two children are in the Story Time area, following the text as they listen to a book on tape. Other children are in the publishing center, working on stories or putting together shopping lists. The writing is uneven and crooked (Cherkasky-Davis shuns lined paper as limiting to free expression) but clearly writing, nevertheless. A girl writes, "Please WrIte Me a letteR," along with her address. Another girl browses through a stack of magazines, doing "research" on just how a magazine is put together.

Of course, some children choose activities unrelated to reading or writing. Two boys in the transportation center guide toy cars across an expansive road map. These children, Cherkasky-Davis says, have, as yet, expressed little interest in writing, always choosing to play in the transportation center. "So what I do is occasionally situate myself over there," she says. "We write traffic tickets and maps of buildings. Then I have them tell me a story about something that happened on the highway. At first, they'd dictate to me and then gradually move into writing."

Hanging around the classroom are children's illustrations of fish. Some are quite elaborate, even dazzling. "We try to integrate everything," Cherkasky-Davis explains. "For the fish unit, we went to the Shedd Aquarium. They had to do research and answer a number of questions. What are fish? What isn't a fish? They later did Japanese fish drawings and paintings of fish. So the unit combined art, math, science, and literature."

Research—having the children discover and analyze information for themselves—is at the center of even the most routine activities at Foundations. The kindergarten children, for instance, take their own attendance, a boy counting the boys and a girl counting the girls before they tally up the total. There is also a number line around the perimeter of the room, and, as the children calculate how many days they have been in school, they walk around the room, trying to identify the correct number.

Because students are assessed on what they can actually do rather than on what they score on an examination, there are no grades at Foundations School. Instead, students are assessed on the basis of portfolios and videotaped performances.

* * * * * * *

After school, Lindy Butler, a friend of Cherkasky-Davis's from another Chicago school, stops by the classroom. An elegant, statuesque African-American woman with gray braided hair, Butler is a twenty-three-year teaching veteran and recent recipient of the prestigious Kohl International Teaching Award, for which Cherkasky-Davis (a former winner of the Kohl, as well as many other awards) nominated her. The nomination, though, had to overcome a major obstacle: Butler needed the endorsement of her principal.

"When I nominated Lindy, I called the principal," Cherkasky-Davis says, "but he said he wouldn't give her an endorsement. He felt threatened by her. She freely invites parents into her classroom; she is also certified as a principal. I called the Kohl Foundation, and they said that, despite the endorsement of dozens of colleagues, Lindy needed the principal's endorsement. 'I guess that's that,' Lindy said. I said to her, 'Wait a minute. To let an administrator stand in your way, for whatever reason, is wrong. You don't stop; you keep pushing. You send in that application and let them send it back.' So Lindy sent in the Kohl application minus the administrator section. They called me and said, 'We can't do this.' I said, 'You can pass up this wonderful teacher, but pass her up because you think she's not the best of the best; don't pass her up because somebody in an administrative capacity doesn't want her to get the award.' And they listened to me because I had a voice. She got the award without the endorsement."

"This is so true," Butler says. "I've told that story a hundred times since I won the Kohl."

The classroom in which the teachers are talking must be approaching a hundred degrees, the sun, slanting through the painted-shut windows, creating brilliant dust motes. It is hard to breathe, so thick is the air. To make matters worse, the telephone, having broken that afternoon, nonsensically rings and rings. No one thinks to unplug it. The teachers are in a conversational groove, swapping stories: there is a story of a principal trying to keep parents out of a school because they lack documentation of a recent tuberculosis test or parent volunteer forms, which no one can find; a story of an administrator denying a teacher's request to let her students visit the Adler Planetarium's mobile Star Lab, even though it is parked out front of the school; and a story of teachers having to make critical personal calls from a pay phone.

Then Butler comes up with an analogy that crystallizes their conversation. "I think we can liken the teachers' movement to the civil right's movement," she says. "For so long, we've been hidden, clamped down on, stepped on. It's hard to step up to someone who has your evaluation in his hands. This is what I'm so thankful to Lynn for. She makes us understand that it has to be our responsibility to make change happen. She empowers us by making us believe that we're good enough to make change happen. If we don't stand up and say we're really good, then all we can do is blame."

There is a thoughtful pause in the conversation. The telephone is still jangling, which perhaps reminds Cherkasky-Davis of one last story: the telephone story. "Teachers don't have phones. You have to go into the office and ask to use it. Well, where I was before I never asked. No one was going to tell me I couldn't use the phone to call about my son or a student. I mean, professionals in other occupations use the phone to call the dentist, while a teacher has to stand in the office begging like a bad girl. Anyhow, when I came here, we wrote a grant for a telecommunications system, and I had a telephone and answering machine installed in my classroom. The principal was leery, afraid that teachers would use the telephone to make personal calls. 'I ask for forgiveness,' I told him, 'not for permission.'"

· · · · · · · ·

At 4 P.M., long after most teachers have gone home, Cherkasky-Davis drives across the city to Pulaski School, where she will conduct a seminar on whole language for elementary teachers. She conducts dozens of seminars, workshops, and training sessions during the course of the year for organizations as diverse as the Illinois Writing Project and the Illinois State Board of Education. While she sometimes receives remuneration as a consultant, some events, such as this one, she does gratis.

With a vita that runs to ten pages, it is easy to think of Cherkasky-Davis as a compulsive workaholic. Juggling both teaching and administrative duties, she often seems overextended. At her desk, papers are piled several inches high. Near the top of the heap is a half-buried paycheck stub.

But Cherkasky-Davis insists she will not give up teaching to become a full-time facilitator, consultant, or anything else. Nor will she, at least for the foreseeable future, be content solely as a classroom teacher. For she is a woman on a mission, and that mission, once again, involves the issue of voice. She feels it is her duty to help teachers discover that they can change what they know is wrong. And she wants teachers to know that it is their responsibility to speak out for what they believe.

In the Pulaski library, Cherkasky-Davis asks the teachers a series of questions: Do their students read real literature as opposed to basals? Do they write and publish their own work? Do the older children read to the younger ones? Do the teachers' classrooms have learning centers?

The teachers respond hesitantly. While some have tried to incorporate whole language into their lessons, there are the familiar problems. Too little planning time. Test scores to worry about. The need to maintain order in the classroom. One teacher sums up the troublesome issues. "We were trained in the old method," she says. "It's going to be a long, long haul. The system, after all, doesn't support whole language, and you have to have the system support you."

"You have to decide if you want to go out on a limb," Cherkasky-Davis says.

Another teacher expresses doubts about the entire whole language enterprise. "I don't think students should always be reading for enjoyment," she says. She is also a proponent of tracking. "The higher kids," she maintains, "shouldn't have to teach the lower kids."

Cherkasky-Davis does not attempt to refute the woman. Instead, she patiently sets out some of the tenets of the whole language philosophy. She knows that effecting lasting change is a long, arduous process. But she is in it for the long haul.

David Ruenzel

• • • • • • •

The Foundations School almost fell victim to Chicago budget cutting at the beginning of the 1993–94 school year. But an outpouring of support from parents and heavy lobbying by Lynn Cherkasky-Davis and her fellow teachers persuaded district officials not to cut the school's already small staff. Early in 1994, Cherkasky-Davis was looking for a larger home for the school's growing enrollment.

♦ ♦ ♦ ♦ ♦ ♦ ♦

Steve Goldstein

This chapter originally appeared as an article in *Teacher Magazine*, November 1993.

11

• •

California Dreamer

Christine Gutierrez

Cudahy, California, is one of those small cities southeast of Los Angeles that even most southern Californians are only vaguely aware of. Bordered by the city of Bell to the north, South Gate to the south, Huntington Park to the west, and Bell Gardens to the east, the city is part of an area characterized by the *Los Angeles Times* as "California in a microcosm: dead factories, a lot of immigrants, gangs, poverty, crowded schools." With a population of about twenty-three thousand packed into 1.1 square miles, Cudahy ranks as the third densest city in Los Angeles County. It is also poor: according to the 1990 census, 27.4 percent of its residents live below the poverty level. From 1980 to 1990, Cudahy's Hispanic population increased by 62 percent, while its Anglo population decreased by 61 percent. It is now about 90 percent Hispanic. One could live a lifetime in Cudahy and not speak a word of English.

This is where Christine Gutierrez has come to help create a "break the mold" school. As she arrives at the Elizabeth Street Learning Center, one of Cudahy's five schools (the city is served by the massive Los Angeles Unified School District), it is not yet 10:00 on an August morning and already the temperature is in the high eighties, and the air is in the "unhealthful" range. Gutierrez is wearing a red blouse, faded black slacks, white socks, and black loafers— casual clothes that make her look younger than her thirty-eight years. She has the kind of energy about her that can only be described as "boundless." Fresh from a two-week visit with her sister in Colorado, Gutierrez seems eager to get back to work. And make no mistake about it: there is plenty of work to be done.

As it is for many of its residents, Cudahy is new territory for Gutierrez. Although she lives in Santa Monica, her "home" for the last five years has been Thomas Jefferson High School in South Central Los Angeles, where she teaches in the school's highly regarded "Humanitas" program. Since the fall of 1992, however, Gutierrez also has taken a leading role in shaping the Los Angeles Learning Centers, one of eleven innovative projects nationwide selected by the New American Schools Development Corporation (NASDC) to "reinvent" America's schools.

A nonprofit organization created in 1991 by business leaders at the behest of President Bush, NASDC has so far pledged $5.7 million to help fund the learning centers, which will serve students in prekindergarten through twelfth grade. The Elizabeth Street School, which previously served 1,600 students in prekindergarten through seventh grade, was selected to become the first center; after a transition period in the fall of 1993, it will officially begin operating as the Elizabeth Street Learning Center—although the new name is already being used. (The site of the second learning center has not yet been announced.)

As Elizabeth Street's curricular coach/lead teacher, Gutierrez will have her hands full in the coming months. But first she must get comfortable in her new surroundings. She has met most of her colleagues, but she is still trying to learn some names. So it is not surprising when, as she enters the school building, she calls the receptionist Marcie instead of Angie. Realizing her mistake, Gutierrez quickly apologizes and then proceeds to Vice Principal Mary Stallings' office, where the teacher receives a warm welcome. Eddie Muñoz, who teaches seventh and eighth grade, stops by to say hello. A former high school teacher, Muñoz transferred to Elizabeth Street just so he could participate in the learning center project. "It's a school," he says, "where I can be innovative and creative and know that I have the support of the administration."

Gutierrez makes her way to the mail room, where she finds a note in her box from one of the teachers. It says:

> Cris,
>
> After two weeks of school, we have come to a con-clusion. We need money. Big money. Can you help us with grant writing or something?
>
> Monica

Gutierrez, who has written numerous grant proposals to help supplement Jefferson High's Humanitas program, files the note away; she seems pleased that her advice is being solicited. After all, her entire career has been about empowering herself as a teacher, and she is eager to see other teachers experience the feeling for themselves.

· · · · · · ·

The word that comes closest to describing Christine Gutierrez is *outspoken*. Asked whether she is more of an activist than a teacher, she replies, "For me, you can't separate the two." Her heroes include such freethinkers as Mahatma Gandhi, John Dewey, and Howard Gardner. "I've always been attracted to people like Thoreau," she says, "people who were willing to take risks."

It is ironic that Gutierrez, a strong advocate of public education, is herself a product of private schools. The granddaughter of Mex-ican-American immigrants, she grew up in a large family in the affluent community of Pacific Palisades, a world away from South Central or Cudahy. From kindergarten through twelfth grade, she attended parochial schools, graduating (as valedictorian) from Marymount High School in Westwood in 1973. These schools have had a lasting influence on Gutierrez, particularly on her thoughts about education. "I think what private schools have to offer is a family orientation," she says, "that very distinct sense of community. You don't just go to a school; you belong to that school."

As a student at Stanford University, Gutierrez created her own interdisciplinary major, Renaissance studies, and immersed herself in academia. Yet she dropped out after three years and returned to Los Angeles. "Being at Stanford was wonderful," she says, "but I needed some time to step back from the academic world. I needed to get into the community and work."

For a while, she worked as an editor at a Santa Monica law firm, exploring the possibility of becoming a lawyer. The law, however, was "intellectually stimulating but emotionally void." She realized she wanted to work with kids, so she quit the job at the law firm and began coaching volleyball at her former elementary school.

At the same time, Gutierrez, a pacifist, was becoming more and more involved in the nuclear-freeze movement, which was then gaining momentum in the politically charged atmosphere of Santa Monica. Working as a volunteer, she lobbied, canvassed, protested, and licked postage stamps—"everything from putting out the trash to answering the phones."

By 1987, Gutierrez had come to the conclusion that, although she loved being a volleyball coach, she wanted to work with kids in a different setting: in the classroom. So she returned to Stanford, first completing her undergraduate degree (her thesis: "Thomas More's Utopia: Simplicity and Human Growth") and then earning a master's degree in education, with credentials to teach English and social studies. She fielded offers from a number of schools, including Marymount, her alma mater. "But that was too easy," she says. Gutierrez knew she wanted to teach in the inner city, and she knew she wanted to teach in a school where teachers were encouraged to work closely with their colleagues. "I wanted intellectual rigor within a collaborative atmosphere," she says. "I didn't want to be just an isolated teacher." She had heard about the Humanitas program at Thomas Jefferson High School, which sits in one of Los

Angeles's toughest neighborhoods. For Gutierrez, there was never any doubt: this was the school for her.

Once a predominantly black high school (among its graduates are such noted African Americans as choreographer Alvin Ailey, actor Woody Strode, singer and actress Dorothy Dandridge, jazz musician Dexter Gordon, and Nobel Peace Prize winner Ralph Bunche), Jefferson High now serves about 3,300 students, 90 percent of them Hispanic. The school is an art deco gem that has been used as a backdrop in numerous movies and television shows. Yet it is like an oasis in the desert, a desert made up of tired-looking bungalows and graffiti-covered walls. A few blocks away, on a small commercial strip, you can still see the burned-out reminders of the 1992 riots (which Gutierrez prefers to call "uprisings").

Gutierrez had her concerns about working in an area known more for its gangs than for its schools. When she first saw the neighborhood, she was riding a bus on her way to her job interview. (For years, Gutierrez was one of the few people in Los Angeles who, for ecological reasons, actually chose not to own a car. Recently, however, after some soul-searching, she broke down and bought a pickup truck.) Looking out the window, she wondered what she had gotten herself into. When she stepped off the bus, she followed a group of teenage girls who were on their way to summer school at Jefferson. Listening in on their conversation, Gutierrez was relieved to hear them talking about the usual things teenage girls talk about: boys and parties. "They were just ordinary kids," she says.

Gutierrez got the job, and, in September 1988, she began teaching history in the Humanitas program. A school within a school, Humanitas is an interdisciplinary, thematic, writing-based curriculum designed to provide students with the kind of enriched academic program more typical of private schools. The goal, according to program literature, is to help students become "critical thinkers, responsible problem solvers, intelligent articulators, and socially conscious community members." Teachers in the program work together to create core courses, which are organized around central themes: "Women,

Race, and Social Protest," for example. Although they must adhere to state and district guidelines, Humanitas teachers are given a great deal of freedom in deciding how they will meet those goals.

Humanitas was launched in 1986 in several Los Angeles high schools, and it has since spread to thirty-six of the district's fifty-two comprehensive high schools. Much of the program's financial support has come from the Los Angeles Education Partnership, the nation's oldest and largest public education fund, along with a handful of private foundations.

At Jefferson, about five hundred of the school's students take part in Humanitas. To get into the program, interested students must fill out a single-page application, which asks such questions as, "What type of books/magazines/newspapers do you like to read?" and "Are you willing to work very hard (including homework every night) to have excellent attendance, to be motivated to study and learn, and to achieve success in this nationally recognized program?"

The cross section of students, Gutierrez says, "is meant to be heterogeneous. So we draw on kids with fourth grade reading levels all the way up to twelve-plus, gifted and talented. We do not look at grades." Until recently, she says, almost everyone who applied to Humanitas at Jefferson was accepted, but last year they had to turn away about 20 percent.

For students who are used to a traditional classroom environment, Humanitas can come as something of a shock. "We're not looking for just regurgitation of facts," Gutierrez says. "We're also looking for conceptual understanding, elegance of style—and that's not just in writing. So it's hard for some kids to accept. They have to perform in a lot of ways that they're not used to performing. It's not enough for them to be brilliant in discussion."

Gutierrez, who is also assistant coordinator of the program, refers to her students and colleagues in Humanitas as a "family," which is not to say that everyone gets along with each other all the time. "Typically," she says, "the kids are attracted to the way we relate to them. But it's not lovey-dovey by any means. We can be harsh with them, brutal sometimes."

Tony Zepeda, a friendly seventeen-year-old with an intense gaze and a buzz haircut, credits Humanitas with helping him grow "both emotionally and socially."

"Before," he says, "when people talked to me, I would stumble and stutter. I wouldn't know what to say. I would just be confused. But now, I've learned how to speak, and I've learned how to analyze. And I've learned how to utilize what I say."

Several years ago, Tony joined a gang. "All my friends were doing it," he says, "and I just wanted to be a part of it." But when he saw one of his best friends shot to death, "cold-blooded," he gave up the gang life. Recently elected Jefferson's student body president, the twelfth grader has found a sense of identity in the Humanitas program. "This is a place where I can let everyone know how I feel," he says. "This is a place where I can be me."

Pamela Aschbacher, project director at the Center for the Study of Evaluation at the University of California at Los Angeles, conducted a three-year study of Humanitas. In a summary published in *Educational Leadership* magazine, she wrote:

> Evidence from surveys, interviews, and assignments suggests that Humanitas teachers assign harder work, expect more from students, and require more complex thought in class discussions and unit essays than comparison teachers. Yet Humanitas students like school better than comparison students, even though they find it demanding.
>
> Several students noted in interviews that they could "probably be getting easy A's in the 'cake bake' classes" but that they preferred to be working harder for B's in Humanitas. The reason? They say they believe they'll learn more and that the experience will help them get into college and do well. In addition, they feel their Humanitas teachers and fellow students care far more about them than comparison students think their teachers and classmates do.

The program has been successful with a diverse population of students, including those who are just learning English and those who have already failed courses
and seem likely to drop out of school. As one teacher put
it, "This program motivates students who would otherwise tune out."

Humanitas teachers, Aschbacher concluded, get as much out of
the program as do the students: "Being a Humanitas teacher requires
a lot of effort. Teachers who participate in the program must learn a
portion of one another's subjects in order to create an interdisciplinary program, develop themes and curriculums, collaborate with
colleagues on a daily basis to coordinate instruction, and grade performance-based assignments. And yet, they almost unanimously
report that participating in Humanitas is one of the most renewing
experiences they have had. . . . That the program creates a community of scholars within the larger, impersonal school context is
critical to its success."

Even the best enterprises, it seems, have their critics, and some
administrators, Gutierrez points out, have not been so keen on the
Humanitas program. "I can't really say it's been malicious," she says.
"It's been more of a subtle power issue. It's teacher led, right? So it's
out of the hands of the administrators." Also, some non-Humanitas
teachers have been resentful of the program. "They have, in the past,
been frustrated with us, thinking, 'You guys get whatever you want,'
forgetting it's not an issue of our getting whatever we want—we just
won't take no for an answer. Our bottom line is, is it good for the
kids? Which means, at times, we break the rules. We break a lot of
rules, including the hierarchical rules. We have no bones about going
to the superintendent, about walking into offices, about hassling
people. . . . We're known to be very outspoken, to be rabble-rousers."

Gutierrez is the first to admit that teaching in the Humanitas
program can be extremely demanding. "It is definitely much more
than a job," she says. After a difficult first year, during which her

classroom was vandalized five times, she began showing signs of burnout. By spring of her second year, she was "completely burned out emotionally and physically.

"I didn't feel that I was focused enough," she says. "I'm not the kind of person who can give halfway. . . . I had so many things going on." She decided to take a three-and-a-half-week, unpaid leave of absence. She saw a lot of movies, read a lot of books, did a lot of crossword puzzles, and spent a lot of time with her husband, Randy Ziglar. "Mostly," she says, "I got quiet and tried to reconnect with who I am and what I really wanted to do."

During that time, Gutierrez was asked to give the commencement speech at Marymount High School. "I was really touched and honored," she says. "But it was so ironic for it to be coming in the period when I was saying, 'Am I failing? Am I on the right track?'"

She began thinking about what she would say in her speech, and, as her thoughts began to crystallize, she realized that she had been too hard on herself, that she had not given herself "permission to fail" during her first two years of teaching. She returned to Jefferson, ready to give it another try.

On a sunny day in late May 1990, Gutierrez looked out at Marymount's graduating seniors, a "sea of smiles," and hinted at the period of reflection she had recently gone through. "The mind is an organism, meant to evolve," she said. "As one is thinking, one is acting and, thus, growing. . . . Growth is the essence of education. To [John] Dewey, the good person is the one who continues to grow, continues therefore to give of oneself. Dewey wrote, 'The good man is the man who, no matter how morally unworthy he has been, is moving to become better. Such a conception makes one severe in judging himself and humane in judging others.'"

Gutierrez urged the students to "question the status quo; question assumptions; question your needs and the needs of society, the needs of the planet. . . .

"It is not enough that you have successfully learned your lessons in the classroom throughout your Marymount years—you need to connect those lessons with how you act outside the classroom in your community, at home, at work, at play. You need to have the courage to act on those lessons now."

Gutierrez told the seniors "to be aware of the consequences of your actions and to take responsibility for your choices," and then she went on to defend a choice she had made, a choice she had recently questioned and then reaffirmed.

"The truth is, I teach in the inner city because there my values are tested, and I am forced to give more of myself. . . . The inner city is fraught with violence, drive-by shootings, crack houses, down-trodden storefronts, littered streets, and graffiti-covered walls. Yet, South Central Los Angeles, like Westwood, is also teeming with life, stirring with potential, full of promise. Celebrating life; that is why we are here. We celebrate life best by renewing it with our gifts."

* * * * * * *

By the time the Los Angeles Educational Partnership decided to take part in the NASDC competition, the deadline—February 14, 1992— was only four months away. Initially, about 150 parents, teachers, community activists, and business leaders ("a panoply of people," Gutierrez says, "many of whom had never talked with one another about education") met in the Atlantic Richfield Co. building in downtown Los Angeles to map out a vision for the future. Gutierrez, along with other Humanitas teachers, was among those who had been asked to attend the meeting.

"We weren't interested in merely creating handbooks for teachers," Gutierrez says. "We really wanted to break the mold. . . . It was an opportunity for a lot of different people in Los Angeles to sit down and really examine how we're educating our young people."

To help make the process easier, eight task forces were created to deal with the major issues: assessment, curriculum, parent involvement, health and social services, technology, governance, professional development, and facilities. Gutierrez was asked to cochair the committee on assessment. The groups met once a week for three-hour sessions, creating, Gutierrez says, "reams of paper."

"We had no preconceived ideas, and we didn't have a guru," Peggy Funkhouser, president of the LAEP, told the *Los Angeles Times*, "but what we came up with represents an amazing amount of consensus."

It was Funkhouser who asked Gutierrez to join the project's nineteen-member design team, a diverse body that included such educational heavies as William Anton, superintendent of the Los Angeles Unified School District; Helen Bernstein, president of United Teachers–Los Angeles, the teachers' union; and Guilbert Hentschke, dean of the University of Southern California's school of education. Gutierrez was the team's only teacher. "I felt humbled," she says. "I had only been teaching for four years. I still thought of myself as the new kid on the block."

Four months after that initial meeting, the consortium (now made up of the LAEP, the school district, the teachers' union, Atlantic Richfield, Bank of America, GTE California, Rockwell International, and the Times Mirror Co.) had its proposal, a one-inch thick document rich with school reform ideas. The proposal called for integrating a number of different concepts over a five-year period at two test sites. Among the most significant components:

- *Educator as continual learner.* Teachers are to be allocated the equivalent of a day a week for professional development, for planning with other teachers, and for meeting with students.

- *"Moving Diamond" concept.* Each student will be matched with a younger student, an older student, a teacher, and a parent or community volunteer, creating a "diamond" matrix that will stay in place for several years. The rationale: "Focus on the individual is sharpened, and every student will know he or she has a stake in someone else."

- *In-depth thematic teaching.* As they do in the Humanitas program, students will attend interdisciplinary
classes for large blocks of time, creating portfolios and
working on long-term projects.

- *Community as classroom and resource.* "The 'egg car-
ton' classroom dominated by a teacher-lecturer with
tedious textbook exercises is our own stereotype of
school. By using the entire community as a source of
intellectual and personal growth, we [will] break this
ancient mold."

In addition, the proposal called for the integration and linking
of health and social services, a strong emphasis on technology, a
clearly defined set of learning outcomes for each subject, and a
"transition to work" program for students in their final two years of
high school.

The consortium asked NASDC for enough money, approxi-
mately $18.5 million, to fund the learning centers through the
1996–97 school year.

Having met the February 14 deadline, the consortium members
waited patiently for NASDC to sift through the submissions—all
686 of them—and make a decision.

Sometime in mid June, Gutierrez got a phone call from Funkhouser. "This is confidential," she said. "NASDC wants to interview
us. We are one of the finalists. Helen [Bernstein] can't go, but she
asked that you go in her place."

Gutierrez had less than a week to prepare for the presentation,
which was to take place on June 19 in Arlington, Virginia, at NAS-
DC's office in the USA Today building. "I really had to do a lot of
homework," she says, "because I was the one who was going to speak
on curricular matters, on what was going to happen in the classroom." Funkhouser would be there, along with Andrew Cazares, an
assistant superintendent for the Los Angeles Unified School District.

Not wanting to miss any more school than she had to, Gutierrez took a red-eye flight to Washington, D.C., the night before the interview was to take place. She arrived at National Airport at 6 A.M., took a cab to an Arlington hotel, checked in, took a two-hour nap, and then met her two colleagues in the hotel lobby. It was the first time they had all met together, face-to-face; Funkhouser had met with both Gutierrez and Cazares, individually, but Gutierrez and Cazares had never met.

They had no idea what the interview would be like. How many people would be there? How long would it last? What would the room look like? "We didn't know anything," Gutierrez says.

In the lobby, they agreed on which aspects of the proposal each of them would be responsible for, then they all went back to their rooms for some last-minute cramming. After a quick lunch, they took a cab to the USA Today building for what turned out to be an "intense" three-hour interview. "They grilled us," Gutierrez recalls, "but we knew we were blowing them away." Still, she had doubts about whether they would actually win the grant.

After it was over, Gutierrez went straight to the airport to catch a flight back to Los Angeles. "I slept all the way home," she remembers.

A few weeks later, Gutierrez was at a meeting in Boston when she got a "frantic" phone call from Funkhouser's assistant. "Where have you been?" she asked. "We've been trying to reach you! They want you in Washington tomorrow." NASDC had selected the learning center project as one of the eleven winning designs.

Gutierrez was thrilled but also nervous about the work that lay ahead. "It was clearly one of those cases of 'Be careful what you wish for,'" she says.

◆　◆　◆　◆　◆　◆

Back in Los Angeles, Peggy Funkhouser urged Gutierrez to become full-time director of the learning center project. But Gutierrez could not bring herself to give up teaching in her beloved Humanitas program, so she ended up splitting the job with design team member Harry Handler, a former superintendent of the Los Angeles Unified School District who is now assistant dean at the UCLA Graduate School of Education. Gutierrez, Handler, and a core group of design team members met regularly to chart a course for implementing the project.

Their first task: selecting a school that would become the first learning center. For one thing, it had to be an inner-city school that could easily be converted to a K–12 facility. And it had to have a staff that was willing to throw preconceived notions out the window.

The Elizabeth Street School fit the bill. In January 1993, Gutierrez and other design team members attended a faculty meeting at the school to make the case for the project. A week later, the teachers voted fifty-four to six to implement the plan. Those teachers who did not want to participate were given the chance to transfer to other schools in the district.

Since then, it has been "one giant jigsaw puzzle" setting up the learning center, says Mike Shannon, a school psychologist who is coordinating the project's health and human services components. "We'll be a different school in January."

This fall, Gutierrez is dividing her time between Jefferson High, where she is teaching two Humanitas classes, and Elizabeth Street, where, as curricular coach/lead teacher, she is helping the teachers write the curriculum they will begin using in January. (Although she is still on the design team, Gutierrez is no longer codirector of the learning center project; in May 1993, Roberta Benjamin, a former school principal, was named full-time director.)

Helping Gutierrez put all the pieces in place at Elizabeth Street are three additional lead teachers, including Anola Hubbert, who has taught at the school since 1985. "I feel very fortunate to be involved in this," she says. "I really do." Hubbert was on the verge of quitting her job and moving to Arizona when she found out about the learning center project. "I felt that I needed a new challenge. I needed something different. And when this came along, I said, 'There's no way I can leave now.'"

Hubbert offers nothing but praise for Gutierrez. "She's fantastic," she says. "Cris is the type of person who makes me want to give 150 percent. She's really dedicated to making this program work. . . . She has so much energy."

If energy were all it took to create a "break the mold" school, the Elizabeth Street Learning Center would already be a success. But Gutierrez is smart enough to know that it takes a lot more. One thing that she worries about is the money. NASDC has reportedly raised only about $55 million of its original $200 million goal, a target that was recently lowered to $100 million. In addition, two of the original eleven projects have lost NASDC support. NASDC is now negotiating contracts with the remaining nine projects one year at a time.

"I'm not sure what's going to happen," Gutierrez says. "Is it fair to ask a lot of people to shift things around and then pull the carpet out from under them?" She hopes that, even if all the funding doesn't come through, much of the project will remain in place. At the moment, plans to open a second learning center in July are still on track.

What impact the learning centers will have on the beleaguered Los Angeles Unified School District is anybody's guess. Lately, the project has been overshadowed by the Los Angeles Educational Alliance for Restructuring Now, or LEARN, a sweeping plan to raise student achievement by shifting decision making to local schools. Although opposed by some teachers, the plan (now being implemented in thirty-six schools, including Elizabeth Street) is seen by many as the district's best chance for improving its schools. (A measure to break up the school district into at least seven smaller units died in the state legislature last July.)

Meanwhile, California voters in November will decide the fate of a plan that would grant vouchers to parents who wish to send their children to private or parochial schools. Education policy makers across the country are anxious to see whether Californians embrace the initiative. After all, as Harold Hodgkinson, director of the Center for Demographic Policy, once wrote, "Leap with joy, be blithe and gay/ Or weep my friend with sorrow./ What California is today/ The rest will be tomorrow."

Christine Gutierrez is doing her best to see that the future of Cudahy—and thus, the future of California—is a little bit brighter. "We're trying to do a hell of a lot in a short time," she says, "and I just don't know if we're going to be able to pull it off. But we'll do our damnedest."

David Hill

• • • • • • •

As of January 1994, Christine Gutierrez was splitting her time between Humanitas classes at Thomas Jefferson High School and curricular duties at the Elizabeth Street Learning Center. The financial outlook for the Elizabeth Street program improved dramatically in December 1993 when philanthropist Walter Annenberg announced a $50 million grant to the New American Schools Development Corporation.

． ． ． ． ． ． ．

This chapter originally appeared as an article in *Teacher Magazine*, November 1993.

. . . .

12

Resolved: Change the System!
Roundtable Discussion

Following is an edited transcript of a discussion held in May 1993 in New York City. The twelve educators who participated are members of the National Re:Learning Faculty, a group of more than a hundred teacher-leaders who work with some five hundred schools around the country to deepen their commitment to the principles of the Coalition of Essential Schools. These teachers are also known as Citibank Faculty because their work is supported by a grant from that corporation. The participants were as follows:

Pat Averette, O'Farrell Community School, San Diego

Steve Cantrell, Rancho San Joachin Middle School, Irvine, California

Bill Chaffin, Weaver High School, Hartford, Connecticut

Karen Coleman, Perryville (Arizona) High School

Cheri Dedmon, Hixson (Tennessee) High School

Marian Finney, Walbrook High School, Baltimore

Lisa Hirsch, University Heights High School, New York

Tony Hoffmann, Middle College High School, Long Island City, New York

Simon Hole, Narragansett Pier School, Narragansett, Rhode Island

Bil Johnson, Bronxville (New York) High School

Carol Lacerenza, The Rippowam Center, Stamford, Connecticut

John Larmer, Oceana High School, Pacifica, California

Paula Evans, director of the National Faculty, arranged the round table. *Teacher Magazine* editor Ronald Wolk asked the questions.

Editors: How serious are the problems in America's schools? How accurate are the appraisals by the media, legislators, and policy makers? Do they justify the kinds of actions being proposed—the massive overhaul being suggested, breaking the mold, starting from scratch, systemic reform?

Bil Johnson: I work in a very nice suburban district where all the kids who graduate go to college. But are these kids really prepared for what the twenty-first century is going to bring? There are a lot of schools and a lot of teachers who don't realize that we are using a hundred-year-old structure to prepare people for the next century. So some basic things such as curriculum, the structure of the day, the size of schools need to change. The real question is whether the system and structures we're working in really work. I don't think they do, even in my nice little suburban school.

John Larmer: Our school is a small suburban school. On the surface, things seem pretty good, but underneath the kids are really hurting, and they're really needy—much more so than when I was in school. That is something restructuring is trying to address. A lot of teachers feel like things are going OK if their classrooms are running smoothly and the kids are doing the work. But I wonder if the kids are really learning what the teachers think they're learning. Or are they really just parroting things back and getting good grades? If so, what does that grade really mean?

Lisa Hirsch: I wish there were more coverage of the good things going on, of course. And there really are a lot of great things going on. But the situation is as bad as they say, if not worse.

Cheri Dedmon: If you ask how the schools are doing, it depends on compared with whom and what. What standard are you going to use to measure schools? That's where we're really inconsistent. We need to ask the question, "Are kids using their minds well?" My school is a national school of excellence and has more than its share of National Merit Scholars. People in the community would ask, "Why would you want to change? You're doing such a good job." But kids aren't being taught to use their minds well. Even our best kids are memorizers; they spit it back out to you. They play the game well, but they can't stand independently and put forth a judgment or defend it or demonstrate reasoning or thinking. That's what we all have in common in our schools. It's frustrating because it is hard to get those top kids to buy into doing anything different. Change is as difficult for kids as it is for the teachers.

Tony Hoffmann: The problems in education are larger than people are saying they are. Anybody who really wants to look at how big the problems are has to look at the situation on two levels, and, on both levels, it's a disaster. The two-parent biological family, with the original parents in that household, is becoming rare. There's a real breakdown in society, and now the schools are being asked to deal with the results. And the schools are totally unequipped and, to some degree, incapable and unwilling to deal with this. When you consider that you need two parents to bring up one child, the school with fifteen to thirty students for each teacher can't do it, no matter how nurturing it is. That is an impossible ratio, given the problems in society. In my middle-class district, I can't tell you how many single, working parents are raising their kids. Many of them don't get home till 6 P.M.

Bill Chaffin: It's an issue of standards and an issue of assessment. Until we start looking at what our standards are for kids—and they are very low—until we start looking for higher standards and assessing them in different ways, you're going to get a majority of people telling you everything is OK, that we're overstating the problem. Because according to the traditional standards and the way they're assessed, through standardized test scores, we're not doing that badly. SAT scores fell significantly during the 1970s and 1980s, but they are rising. People would point to that as evidence that we're doing OK, and a good number of our students are going to college. But we shouldn't be judging our students on that basis. We need to change how we judge our students and how we test them. When we do that, people will start to look at students and say, "We're not doing the job."

Simon Hole: Let me offer the metaphor of the manual typewriter. We can fine-tune it and make it work a little bit better, but it is never going to be a word-processing system. The problem in education is worse than people think because they have in mind taking that typewriter and refining it and maybe getting another ten words a minute out of it. But that kind of tinkering will never make the system what it really needs to be. We need to change traditional structures and classroom practice to get kids to think and use their minds. But we've also got to change the culture of the school. We need to break the isolationism that is so apparent in the classrooms and in the lives of school people. We need to create collegial schools of continuous improvement. The structural changes, the individual classroom practice changes won't last unless we change the culture of the entire school.

Marian Finney: Education is in worse condition than people say it is. And teachers have to acknowledge that. We really have to change our paradigms before we can expect to make any meaningful changes in the education system.

Editors: Sounds like it's unanimous. All of you think the problems in schools are as bad or worse than the media and policy makers say they are.

Cheri Dedmon: If everything's as bad as we say it is, it's pretty amazing that things are working at all. Gosh, maybe there are some places where it's working in spite of all the problems. It's amazing that kids are coming out with anything. Maybe there's something positive happening.

Editors: Children who bring a great deal with them to the classroom are likely to do well or at least survive irrespective of the quality of the school, as long as the school doesn't hurt them. The question is whether schools are adding value.

Bil Johnson: You see that when kids leave school, in terms of how much retraining corporations have to do, how much remediation colleges have to do in the freshman year. I bristle at the idea that kids are surviving, so the system's fine. There's an analogy in the Fosbury flop. Everybody for years and years high jumped a certain way. Then all of a sudden, this guy, Dick Fosbury, starts running at the bar and does it completely differently and sets new records. It totally changed the way everybody since has done it. We are talking about going over the bar in a totally different way.

Bill Chaffin: I've heard the term *twenty-first century* mentioned a number of times—preparing our kids to go out into a new century. I don't think people are clear, and I include myself in that category, about what's different now from the way it was in the fifties, sixties, and seventies. People aren't clear about what the expectations are for our students and how we have to prepare kids differently to meet new demands.

Editors: When you say "people," whom are you talking about?

Bill Chaffin: People in the communities. Our own colleagues. I don't think they have a sense of what companies are looking for in terms of workers, what colleges are looking for in terms of students, and how that's changed. Industry is changing and is requiring a different type of person to do a different type of work. That is going to affect how we educate kids. Many people are not really aware of that. They still think you finish high school, and you either go on to college or become a factory worker. If you become a factory worker, this is what you do every day. That's just not the reality any longer. If people don't understand that shift, they will not understand why schools have to change. The system worked so well for them, they think: Why do we want to change it?

Tony Hoffmann: People may not be doing anything about changing, but surely they understand that there are no factory jobs anymore. That's pretty clear; the factory jobs are overseas. The problem is an inability to shift. People are mired in the past. They can look at themselves and say, "I'm not doing well; I have to change, but I'll change tomorrow because it's too hard today." That's what's going on. It's not that they don't realize the world is changing or that they don't know they ought to change; it's a general societal unwillingness to make basic and painful changes.

Editors: You all seem to agree that there are indeed serious problems in our schools, but how about your colleagues? Do they share your view?

Group: (Laughter.)

Pat Averette: My staff realizes that there is a need for change. But what we are finding is that various people think that that change should happen in different ways. It's a problem because there is no map; there's no blueprint for how to restructure successfully. As a result, there is a lot of walking through the dark and bumping into things and saying, "Maybe we should turn here."

Editors: Are you suggesting that a substantial proportion of the present teaching force in the United States does think that there is a need for change?

Group: No.

Carol Lacerenza: In my part of the country, which is not very far from this very big urban center, the consensus is that the clientele needs to change—that as soon as society fixes the kids, my teaching is going to be fine. I'm near a small urban center that is racially and economically divided, and all of the bad teaching is blamed on the portion of our community who does not come to the party with the right equipment. There is not universal acceptance of the notion that we need to change. In fact, there's a universal resistance. There are some little things done and minor adjustments made, but we are still expecting society to give us better kids.

Marian Finney: Teachers who have been teaching longer think there is nothing wrong with their practices; there's something wrong with the students. And teachers who are new to teaching come with no baggage. In Baltimore, we're slowly moving to the point where we realize we do need to change. It's painful, it's time-consuming, but it must happen. Still, there are folks who feel that if they wait long enough, this too will pass, and mothers will send me better children or something else will happen. Some magic wand will be waved. Teachers may realize something must happen, but it doesn't necessarily have to happen to them.

Simon Hole: Pat's "walking through the dark" statement is exactly what it feels like. And, unfortunately, the majority of teachers aren't walking—they're paralyzed. It's dark, and to move, even if they recognize that they should be moving, is just too scary. The isolation just makes it too hard. Any moving they do attempt tends to be tinkering around the edges. It's not transformative in any way. Reflective practice is not a norm in most schools. You're too focused on the here and now to look backward at what you did yesterday or to try to look forward to what you can do tomorrow. There's just no time to do anything except to look at where we are right now. So most teachers don't. On the intellectual level, they're aware that change needs to happen; but on a gizzard level, it just can't be done. There's not enough time.

Lisa Hirsch: You really can't make any changes until the whole faculty feels as we do. It's easier for one person to go over the high bar than it is to get thirty teachers in the school moving in the same direction. But change isn't impossible at all when you have a whole group of people working together. It's really not impossible.

Editors: If you start with the assumption that no significant, enduring change is likely to occur without a substantial majority of the teaching force behind it, then the question becomes, How are we ever going to improve schools? You've sketched out a spectrum of attitudes: there are those who don't realize the need for change; there are some who might accept minor changes but don't realize the need for profound change; there are those who may acknowledge the need for significant change at the intellectual level, but, since they're scared and don't quite know what to do, they're paralyzed. Are there also teachers at the far end of the spectrum who are actively resisting, who have dug in and are ready to fight? If so, what motivates them? How big a problem are they going to be in the effort to really reform schools?

Steve Cantrell: Change for most teachers isn't a new idea; they've been told to change for all of their teaching careers. Some of the most resistant teachers are often people who embraced earlier models of change, and it didn't work out. So they've been burned, and they are angry because they put their hopes in something that didn't work. Then there are those who didn't buy into that particular change, whatever it was, and they pointed their fingers afterward and said, "Told you it wouldn't work." So they're really resistant this time around, as well. They say, "I've seen changes before; they come and go, and this isn't going to work either. I'm not going to be burned like the rest, so I'm going to take myself out of this argument altogether."

Bill Chaffin: Society in general does not see educational reform as one of its priorities and doesn't see teachers as professionals. If we were true professionals, we would be given the time to engage in some reflective practices at school that would make it much easier for people to go through a change process. We're not given that time because it costs money, and taxpayers have to pay for it. The public doesn't think this is really important; the educational health of children is not as important as the medical health of children.

Bil Johnson: That characterizes a lot of people out there who are resistant in one form or another. But the changes teachers have experienced over the last twenty or thirty years have always been mandated from the top down. Changes haven't generated from grass-roots movements of teachers who felt the need for change or thought the school wasn't working. Either the federal government, the state government, or the local district said, "Here's what we're going to change." There was token input from teachers, at best. And the change hasn't been at all connected to real classroom situations. Some of the negative attitudes and resistance result from teachers feeling like we're always being told to make this or that change. In the Coalition of Essential Schools, we're involved in something that is grass-roots and teacher generated to a large extent. But, for many teachers, there are all kinds of reasons not to go along. They will need a lot of administrative support and vision. This is a much more difficult kind of change to implement than things that have happened before.

Lisa Hirsch: It's so incredibly difficult. Even in a school like mine, where the sky is practically the limit, there are still strains on us. I can say to myself, "I'm going to be totally different; I'm going to do this wonderful thing and this and this," but I still have the Regents competency test to contend with, and I have to teach about the Babylonians. We can try a new paradigm, but, when student scores don't go up on standardized tests, people will say, "I told you." And then it's back to the drawing board and no more money for these "foolish little things" that you're trying to do.

Cheri Dedmon: For some teachers, change means moving the desk or rearranging the room; that's a change. Or if they move to another room in the course of their lifetime at school, that's a big change for them. Teachers don't get into the teaching profession because they like change. People get into teaching because they don't like change.

Tony Hoffmann: When I first walked into a classroom, I had no baggage. My colleagues and I were idealistic. I tried everything in my classes and got shot down by the administration, even by parents attached to the old system. Some of us have maintained our idealism, but a lot of people got molded into these intractable people who consider moving to a different room the major change of a lifetime. Somehow schools have to be organized so that people feel comfortable with change rather than comfortable with the status quo.

John Larmer: A whole lot of people go into teaching because they like to be on their own, and they like the independence ("This is my only domain, my classroom"), and so they think, "Why change?" or "Why work with colleagues?" or "Why expand?" They just have a Lone Ranger mentality.

Carol Lacerenza: We're a bit on the radical side in this room. Not everybody wants to reform and restructure all of education from the top down or from the bottom up. A change or two here or there is OK, and, if that's the beginning of the larger change, that'll take place. We need to encourage people to begin somewhere and to help people experience small successes and have the early conversations around the things that can be read and shared. It's OK not to be radical.

Editors: Let's talk for a while about the things that have to be done. You've alluded to problems such as isolation, the culture of the schools, structural problems. Apart from waving a magic wand to improve the children who come to school, what would you do to make schools better?

Bil Johnson: Year-round schools.

Cheri Dedmon: You have to teach teachers how to work with adults. We were trained to work with children. You walk into the classroom, shut the door, and you're the boss; you make all the decisions. If that's going to change, we have to learn how to work with other adults.

Carol Lacerenza: And we have to teach teachers how to take initiative. A lot of teachers did not sign up to take the initiative, to change course.

Bill Chaffin: We have to create situations in our schools where we're teaching kids about the same issues that we're talking about ourselves: what we have to go through to change as teachers and what we have to go through to change schools. All the issues that are involved have to be brought down to the students—not bringing them down as in simplifying them but engaging students in these same issues. Instead of expecting society to change itself so that we have better students, we have to act now to change our classrooms and give our students what they need to change society.

Carol Lacerenza: Teaching as a subversive activity.

Bill Chaffin: Exactly. As I work at team building, as I reflect on practice, I bring it to my own classroom and involve my students. And I find that I can do the same things with my high school students that I do with a group of adults. It makes no difference. They attack the issues the same way adults do and get the same things out of discussions that adults do.

Simon Hole: It goes the other way, too—what we do with kids in the classroom are the same kinds of things we should be doing with our colleagues and with the community. I know a teacher, for example, who does the best job I've ever seen teaching kids how to work in cooperative groups but who had never thought about using those same skills to create a staff that learns how to work together. It's not the norm of the school to do that. So she teaches in isolation, which just strikes me as crazy. We've got to change that somehow.

Karen Coleman: We also need to change our concepts, our ideas of where learning can occur. A lot of people—parents, kids, teachers—come to school with the idea that learning can only occur in the classroom. We need to look at school more as a lab that isn't confined to one structure or one space.

Tony Hoffmann: One of the most important ways of getting kids to succeed is to create schools where they want to be, places that are good for them. We need small schools; large schools are impossible. We create small schools first, and then we create small classes.

There is no single model for what makes successful teaching and learning, but you've got to go with smallness first.

Marian Finney: We must not only make them small and more personal, but we also have to make schools people-friendly and include parents in that picture. Parents must know what we're trying to do in schools, must feel that schools are people-friendly and that they're involved. We need small schools that are attuned to students' needs and parents' needs. Many parents, especially in secondary schools, feel that they no longer need to be part of their child's daily educational endeavors.

Tony Hoffmann: As I go around to different schools, I am impressed with the quality of the teachers. The quality of the teaching staff is very high in this country. The key to reform and restructuring is trust. If there is a sense of trust throughout the school, whether it's the students' trust for the teachers or the teachers' trust for the administration, then things will get done. If there isn't that basic trust, things won't get done. Where there is good leadership, you will find a sense of trust.

Steve Cantrell: Tony's right. It's trust; it's attitude and character and, I would add, honesty. When communities are surveyed as to how they think their schools are doing, they say their own school is fine, but all the others are in trouble. Teachers also tend to think their own school is doing well. But deep down, there's a real fear that if their practice is exposed, they'll be in trouble. Because they work in isolation, they really don't see other teachers' classrooms. They know things aren't perfect in their own classrooms, and they know that they could probably be doing things better. But who are they going to tell if they think that everybody else is doing it right? If there were trust, if there were honesty, teachers could first of all look at themselves and at their own practice and then be able to seek help in the same way that professionals do. They could get together and talk about serious issues that they face in their own practice.

Cheri Dedmon: What we're talking about here, in a sense, is power. Most teachers feel they are powerless in this process. That's ironic considering that they are the people dealing most directly with the children. I don't think that says we don't value education in this society; it says we don't value children. Most teachers feel like the principal has the power. The principal feels like the superintendent does. The superintendent says the school board has the power. The school board says it's the state department of education. So who actually has that power to do all of this? If we can convince teachers that they have the power themselves to make a difference—that one teacher can make a difference—then we have something to build on. But most teachers feel like, "Why should I change?" Or they think that they aren't going to make any difference, that this is going to be the same old thing. So the issues of who has the power and what do we value in our society come back to the classroom. And that's where you see what we do or do not value.

Bill Chaffin: At the classroom level, the basic change would be a curriculum change. What do we teach or what do we think is important? To make systemic change in a school or in a school system, one of the first decisions that has to be made is what are we going to teach kids? What are they going to have to do when they leave school? How are you going to get them there? We need to rethink that.

Editors: Many of the people who are really pushing for systemic reform have the notion that it has got to be curriculum driven. You define what it is you want kids to know and be able to do, you craft a teaching force that knows what it should teach and how to do it, you devise a set of curriculum frameworks that give teachers a tremendous amount of flexibility, and then you develop an assessment program that enables you to really measure whether or not the kids have accomplished and can do what you say they should be able to do. On paper, that makes very good sense; it's very logical. Theoretically, if you could do that, everything else in the system could change—the structure, the calendar, the use of time, the use of space, the relationships between people, the power distribution throughout this system. That's the theory.

Carol Lacerenza: That's all true and very well stated, but the problem comes when people have to decide what they want students to be able to do or know at a given point in the learning process. In order for us to make classroom changes and to make them meaningful in the future lives of these students, we have to have a constant conversation about what it is that's essential for these teachers and students to share. That's a conversation that should never end, but it's difficult to sustain because we are not in the habit of self-analysis. We're not in the habit of baring our souls even to one another because we have this strange idea that there's one right way to teach, that we learned how to be teachers, and this is how you do it. There's great trepidation about a conversation that says, "I really stink at this. I need to think differently about how I can better interact in this particular scenario. Can you help me?" That's a difficult conversation to start, and we can't get at all of those systemic issues until that conversation can thrive.

Pat Averette: I agree; it's about the lack of reflective practice. One thing about being reflective is if you find something wrong, then you have to do something about it. You may have to change. Part of the reason education is in the situation it's in is that we're not accustomed to looking at what we're doing and saying, "Oh, maybe that's not working so well. How do we change that? What's the best way of going about it?" And without that, I don't think it makes a difference what curriculum you're teaching.

Bil Johnson: We've had a conversation about change for the past six years in my school, but it has mostly consisted of one-hour department meetings or monthly faculty meetings. How do you sustain that kind of conversation or really get involved in talking about reflective practice with colleagues if you don't have the time and the structure? People want the quick fix—"You've got nine common principles, put them into practice, and let's see the test scores next year." If you want teachers to be reflective, then you have to give them time to do it.

Simon Hole: Who's in the conversation is really important. We have to work hard to go out and get people who are not in the conversation, who've never been in the conversation. And I'm not talking about our colleagues on the staff—I'm talking about the community. There's a huge risk in that, but, if reform is going to work, everybody has to buy into it. That doesn't mean we have to sell it; it means we have to develop it with everybody.

Editors: Isn't it likely that changing practice would also provide more time for reflection and professional growth? Why shouldn't schools operate like other organizations do? Take a newspaper, for example. Writers have great autonomy. They're responsible for beats. When they are working, they're also learning. Editors supervise, teach, and correct. They make sure that what reporters do is right and that they are staying on course. The people in a newspaper office work every bit as hard as teachers and students do, but, because of the way they work, there is time for communication, interaction, and thinking. If a school functioned more like a newspaper, students would be involved in authentic projects that give them a chance to learn and produce real work. And teachers would work together and with students to oversee and coach students. Wouldn't there be more time? And wouldn't that time be used more productively for everyone?

Lisa Hirsch: Three other teachers and I are advisers to the school newspaper. The students are workers producing the paper, and we get to communicate. We spend hours planning, and then they're off. They are working on a project and learning. They all learned how to use the computer, and they are doing the layout themselves. I have to get a student to teach me what they have learned. And we do start building in time for thought and communication. It still isn't enough time. I don't think there ever will be enough time. Let me mention another change that helps. We use student advisory groups or family groups in our school. Teachers have responsibility for keeping in touch with fifteen or twenty students and being concerned for their welfare in and out of school. That's an incentive to work that much harder. In our school, a teacher stays with a group of students until they graduate, so there's less chance of a student falling through the cracks.

Bill Chaffin: Having an authentic work situation for kids is a nice goal; that's where we should be heading. But we can't send our kids off all the time to work by themselves and then check on them every once in a while. We have to be sure they're mature enough and self-disciplined enough to go out and do that. We have to start putting things in place in school that get kids to the point where they feel that they're responsible for their own behavior, so that you can leave a group of kids to do something and meet with a group of teachers and engage in some kind of reflective practice while the students are working on something else and not worry that something horrendous is happening.

Tony Hoffmann: At Middle College High School, we've been able to restructure the time schedule so that we have the time to communicate. We have professional committees that help set policy. But the main thing is we restructured the school so that there is a time during school hours when there can be extensive dialogue.

Editors: Some people think that the problem in education is that American students are not working hard enough and are not expected to work very hard. Do you agree?

Simon Hole: I see kids in first grade who are naturally curious and have an ability to see a whole picture. And we train that out of them. One of the things that happen is that elementary schools— even in a self-contained, isolated classroom—try, perhaps not even consciously, to become like a high school. Like, "Oh it's 10:15—we have a fifteen-minute spelling lesson now." So we're compartmentalizing stuff in ways that feel like a high school model.

Editors: And is it possible that students lose the desire to work because they're just bored and not interested?

John Larmer: There's no reason for them to work. They can get by with a D average and graduate with a diploma. They're never forced to really show that they can do things. You've got to up the stakes on kids. Get them to give public performances and that kind of thing. The credit system instead of the competency system. We need to get away from the idea of seat time. Kids need to feel that their work is valuable, that they're doing things that are valuable to them, not to some adult.

Carol Lacerenza: Right. Schools aren't really for kids. They're for the adults who are in the schools running them. And they're a place to get kids ready for some artificial next step. Either Algebra II or seventh grade or the test—and that's all artificial, and that has nothing to do with whether students are being asked to think and to engage in meaningful experiences for them. It has to do with teacher measurements. Am I a good teacher if I send those kids off to seventh grade? What will the seventh grade teacher say about me? And how can I prepare my students to be my spokesperson? All kinds of things obstruct that natural curiosity and natural learning because the adults are there for different reasons than they should be.

Bill Chaffin: How are kids' values any different from ours? We talk about kids coming into school and not working hard. Look at society in general. Do we value hard work in society? Look how it's set up. We have this "instant society" where you get most of your information from TV. You don't have to think about it. They tell you what's going on. You see it as it's happening. You don't have to think about it. Why would we be surprised that our kids come into our schools with the same values that we live with every day? I think that we need to start changing society from the school out instead of worrying about changing the society before they come in.

Karen Coleman: What we're talking about is work that's quality. A lot of kids work hard, but they settle for a product that's not a quality product when they could do better. But as long as they get their A or their B or whatever grade that we assign them, then they settle for that. It may not be the best work that they can provide us with.

Cheri Dedmon: What is the definition of work? I see it change for my students, and I guess it's the best change. I've got two sons, fairly young. This fall, we were going to rake leaves—a job I hate. My younger son is just raking and raking and working so hard. The older one comes out, cranks up the blower, and he's done his work in ten minutes, and he's back inside. And I'm thinking, He's using his mind well; he has his technology together. But is he lazy? He got his job finished; he didn't use as much time as we did or as much effort, but he got it done. In other words, he's going to have to find a career one of these days where he can use his mind well because he's not going to do a lot of physical labor. The other child out there raking and raking—now he's going to rake all day long, but he's not questioning. That reminds me of the kids in the classroom. They're doing the drill sheets and the memory sheets. They'll work as long as they need to, and they'll play that game. They'll please the teacher. But are they using their minds well? I see work being defined differently for kids because they come in and say, "Why should I have to go through all these hoops teachers set up for me? If I can get from here to there doing it a different way, why does it matter?" The definition of work for kids is going to change. We don't have to change it for them. They're going to change it for us.

Steve Cantrell: Cheri's story about raking leaves prompted me to think that teachers generally work very hard, but I wonder if they don't spend most of their time raking. We're all talking about creating time for all the things that teachers need to do, the real intellectual work. I don't see a lot of intellectual work on my campus, and I include myself. I think a lot about pedagogical issues but not enough about my own discipline, and that's sort of a choice; that's what my interests are. But if we're not learning, if we're not actively engaged in learning about something, we're hypocritical to think that the kids are going to do what we tell them to do.

Editors: That leads to the subject of teacher professionalism and teaching as a profession. What can teachers do to make teaching more of a profession, irrespective of the system or perhaps despite the system or as part of an effort to change the system?

Bil Johnson: The problem starts with education schools. The focus of teacher training is not on reforming and restructuring. I constantly berate college teaching because I don't think it is teaching. It is a holdover from a medieval system where somebody who could read the book stands there and presents it to the people. And that kind of didactic example is what I hear from people who are going through education school. If we're talking about long-range change, the conversation we're having here today has got to take place in ed schools. We can't continue to turn out generation after generation of teachers who basically are going to say, "Well, this is the way I was taught, so we'll just perpetuate the system and not rattle the cage."

Tony Hoffmann: Instead of getting students as student teachers, we should get the professors as student teachers. They should be the ones who do their year internship with us. Some of them taught a few years a couple of decades ago and haven't been in the classroom since, other than to follow up on their students for an hour or so to tell them what they're doing right or doing wrong. It's very important to establish a much better collaboration between the schools and teaching colleges. And not only should the college teachers become student teachers (I was not being flippant about it), but also teachers in the schools should be in the colleges training the future teachers.

Simon Hole: I don't disagree with the idea that teacher preparation has to change, but you train those kids and give them all these wonderful ideas, and then you're going to put them out into the schools. What happens is they come in and spend that first year or two just being overwhelmed with what's going on in the classroom. If there aren't support systems built in to help those new folks maintain those ideas and ambitions, they're soon gone.

Marian Finney: Support groups are needed for people who are entering the teaching profession. But people who've been teaching for a while must take the initiative to establish reading groups, to be more involved in professional organizations beyond just getting the subscriptions and putting them on the shelf, to do some writing, to develop more of a voice. They have to be more active in the profession, as opposed to letting other people tell them what to do. Teachers are the only professionals who let everybody else in the world tell us what to do, how to do it, and when to do it.

Steve Cantrell: We're talking about teacher training as it happens at the college, but we're forgetting about what happens with that first-year teacher. One of the reasons I took my current position was that it had built into it a structured way for me to continue to develop professionally. There's somebody on the site full time whose only job is currently to develop teachers. And I thought that's a place where I could go and learn. In addition, he directs the professional development on-site, and that's all led by teachers, teachers serving teachers, saying, "What are needs that you have?" Unlike the doctor with a problem who goes to another doctor, we're doing the reverse. We're going out to our people and saying, "We know you have problems."

Group: (Laughter.)

Marian Finney: Teachers have to demand to be considered professionals. That's something that we have to work through and talk about and come to some action plans where we can demand that the public see us as professionals and treat us as such.

Cheri Dedmon: I'd like to see my workday designed a little differently—to be more professional, like at the college level, where you have teaching days, and you maybe have afternoons when you can get together with colleagues or do research or whatever. I'd like to see a different work year, so I'm teaching part of the year and have three to four weeks in between so I can work with somebody on an idea or a plan or go someplace and get renewed. We can't count on changing schools simply by changing the teachers coming into the profession; we've got to change what's there right now.

Simon Hole: Teacher-leaders are asked to do so much. It drove me out of the classroom. I'm on leave because I just couldn't take it anymore. It wasn't fair to the kids. The true culture of most schools has a norm of faculty equality, that all teachers are the same, that the only differentiation comes from seniority, and that's it. Until we begin looking at each other and are able to say, "John, you know stuff that I don't know; help me learn"—until that happens, we're not going to be a profession.

Paula Evans: For most of seventeen years, I taught in an upper-middle-class suburban school—lots of money in the school budget, a parent community that cared enormously, and continues to care, about the education of its kids. I was allowed to do basically whatever I wanted to. And for most of those seventeen years—I've been out of the classroom since 1983—I team-taught my courses. I didn't know the words or the language then, but my courses, as I look back on them now, were exhibition based. I taught kids for three-hour blocks of time at night instead of the four or five periods during the week. I was considered by some of my colleagues to be radical. And I would go to the principal and say, "Look at how this works; isn't it terrific." And he would say, "Yes, it's terrific; continue doing it." But it never spread to the rest of the school.

Recently, I went back to the school after being out of it for ten years. People told me how much the school had changed—my former colleagues, the population, the way people were approaching kids. I figured I needed to go there and look at this place with fresh eyes because I obviously didn't know this school anymore; it's not the school that I taught in. I went in and sat through four classes, and I felt like I had been out for one week with the flu. Nothing had changed about that school; it is as heavily tracked, it is as fragmented, it is as teacher dominated as it always was. And the things that I did that were radical fifteen years ago would still be considered radical today.

I think that those of you around this table are in a different place. I hope you are, and I hope that the coalition helps put you in a different place and gives you authority and leverage to really make a difference. Because what I realized when I came away from that school was that I had some terrific experiences, but I never made a difference to that school. I may be naive, but I hope and feel that you will and can make a difference.

Afterword

—The Editors

The overriding conclusion that we would like readers to take from this book is that the teachers portrayed here have set a standard that is reachable by the majority of American teachers. After all, these people are not superheroes. They have no special powers that set them apart from their colleagues; future generations will not read about them in history books. These teachers are simply people who were dissatisfied with the way things were, who really wanted to do better, and who made the commitment to use their talents and resources to improve their corner of the world.

We can only hope that the day will come when teachers like these are the rule rather than the exception. That day would come sooner if teacher preparation programs produced thinking professionals dedicated to improving the system. Instead, for the most part, these programs simply train workers to fit into it. Of course, more teachers might question the status quo and seek better ways of doing things if the system rewarded initiative and risk taking instead of punishing it.

Undoubtedly thousands and thousands of teachers know that schools can be better and that they can help make them so. We hope these profiles will be an inspiration to them.

—The Editors

DATE DUE

1-3-95			
7/12/96			
APR 1 5 1998			
GAYLORD			PRINTED IN U.S.A.